The Long & Short of It

The Long & Short of It
first published 2018 by Scirocco Drama
An imprint of J. Gordon Shillingford Publishing Inc.
© 2018, the authors

Scirocco Drama Editor: Glenda MacFarlane
Cover design by Terry Gallagher/Doowah Design
Photos on pages 7–10 by Haanita Seval
Photo of Joseph Aragon by Haanita Seval
Photo of Sharon Bajer by Kevin McIntyre
Photo of Rick Chafe by Tim Leyes
Photo of Ginny Collins by Dylan Hewlett
Photo of Trish Cooper by Lucky Girl Photography
Photo of James Durham by John Woods
Photo of Jason Neufeld by Jason Neufeld
Photo of Debbie Patterson by Solmund MacPherson
Photo of Ellen Peterson by Leif Norman
Photo of Alix Sobler by Matthew Dunivan
Photo of Brian Drader by Maxime Cote

Printed and bound in Canada on 100% post-consumer recycled paper.
We acknowledge the financial support of the Manitoba Arts Council and
The Canada Council for the Arts for our publishing program.

All rights reserved. No part of this book may be reproduced, for any reason, by any means, without the permission of the publisher. These plays are fully protected under the copyright laws of Canada and all other countries of the Copyright Union and are subject to royalty. Changes to the text are expressly forbidden without written consent of the author. Rights to produce, film, record in whole or in part, in any medium or in any language, by any group, amateur or professional, are retained by the author.

Library and Archives Canada Cataloguing in Publication

The long & short of it : a selection of short plays written by the Prairie Theatre Exchange Playwrights Unit / edited by Brian Drader.

ISBN 978-1-927922-42-2 (softcover)

1. Canadian drama (English)--Manitoba. 2. One-act plays, Canadian (English)--Manitoba. I. Drader, Brian, 1960-, editor II. Prairie Theatre Exchange (Winnipeg, Man.). Playwrights Unit, author III. Title: Long and short of it.

PS8315.5.M35L66 2018   C812'.0410806   C2018-902109-8

J. Gordon Shillingford Publishing
P.O. Box 86, RPO Corydon Avenue, Winnipeg, MB Canada R3M 3S3

The Long & Short of It

A selection of short plays
written by the
Prairie Theatre Exchange
Playwrights Unit

Edited by Brian Drader

Contents

Foreword by the PTE Playwrights Unit	7
Fare Thee Well, Bob by Sharon Bajer	11
The Chosen One by Joseph Aragon	15
Chess by Sharon Bajer	25
Rage: A Love Story by Rick Chafe	33
The Propeller Moment by Ginny Collins	41
Life of Pie by Trish Cooper	49
Preparing for Field Day by James Durham	57
The Routine by Jason Neufeld	65
On the Money by Debbie Patterson	73
The Intersection by Ellen Peterson	83
Agony & Ecstasy by Alix Sobler	89
Biographies	101

Foreword

Left to right: Playwrights Sharon Bajer and Debbie Patterson, director Ann Hodges, and playwrights Rick Chafe, Trish Cooper, and James Durham, on stage at the 2015 Carol Shields Festival of New Works.

The short plays (Short Shots, as we like to call them) in this anthology were all commissioned by Prairie Theatre Exchange (PTE) for staged readings at the Carol Shields Festival of New Works, and written by us, the PTE Playwrights Unit. They offer a trip down the rabbit hole of our collective consciousness where you'll encounter five-year-olds, zombies, feuding families, homemade pies (or are they?), and cynical tour guides.

Luckily for us, PTE is in the business of adopting playwrights and supporting new works. The Carol Shields Festival and the Playwrights Unit were both founded by PTE under the direction of Artistic Director Bob Metcalfe in 2004 and 2007 respectively. A champion of Canadian work and local writers, Bob is a recipient of the Order of Manitoba, and was awarded the Bra D'Or for his efforts to promote and support the work of Canadian women playwrights. He has commissioned, nurtured and lovingly produced 19 new plays developed through the Playwrights Unit.

Left to right: Actors Doug McKeag, Aaron Pridham,
Dora Carroll and Kimberley Rampersad, staged reading,
The Carol Shields Festival of New Works.

Bob's relentless support and encouragement keeps our pens on the page. He believes in us when we stop believing in ourselves. He even carved out a space for us at PTE by giving us a room and Playwrights' Library. This book is for him.

The members of the PTE Playwrights Unit, past and present, include Joseph Aragon, Sharon Bajer, Rick Chafe, Ginny Collins, Trish Cooper, James Durham, Jason Neufeld, Debbie Patterson, Ellen Peterson, Marc Prescott, Ian Ross, and Alix Sobler. A mix of established and emerging writers, the Unit's purpose is to give local playwrights a home base; a place to collaborate, explore ideas, and access resources while we work on our plays. Monthly meetings consist of scene readings, idea sharing and, most importantly, group therapy. Playwriting is a lonely business, made somewhat less lonely by the presence of people who share in your misery and triumph. Like any good family, we drag each other up and out of the literary muck on a regular basis, and keep each other accountable and grounded.

Over the years, many of our plays, and those of the wider Canadian playwriting community, have been workshopped and developed as part of the Carol Shields Festival of New Works. The festival invites audiences to actively participate in the process through public readings. Plays such as *Armstrong's War* and *Pig Girl* by Colleen Murphy, *The Moonlight Sonata of Beethoven Blatz* by Armin Wiebe, *The Great Divide* by Alix Sobler, *Head* by Debbie Patterson, *Burnin' Love* by Sharon Bajer, *The Secret Mask* by Rick Chafe, *The Brink* by Ellen Peterson, *Social Studies* by

Left to right: Actors Carson Nattrass and Andrea Houssin, staged reading, The Carol Shields Festival of New Works.

Trish Cooper, *The Flats* by Ginny Collins, *How the Heavens Go* by Joseph Aragon and more were developed and given public readings at the festival, and then went on to receive professional productions at PTE or elsewhere. Since its inception, the Prairie Theatre Exchange has produced 151 world premieres.

The Carol Shields Festival is also where Short Shots, such as the ones in this anthology, are born. Each year, five short plays are commissioned by PTE and performed at the festival's gala event. The Carol Shields Gala, which also serves as the opening ceremony for the festival, invites artists from a variety of disciplines including dance, music, spoken word, and more to perform in a cabaret-style program. Over the years, Short Shots have been written by both the PTE Playwrights Unit and members of the wider playwriting community in Manitoba. The writers are asked to use that year's "festival theme" as their inspiration. These short plays provide us with the perfect opportunity to explore ideas, try some new moves, and stretch our writing muscles in a safe setting. Some have even inspired full-length works, including Rick Chafe's *Marriage: A Demolition in Two Acts* and *The Secret Mask*, as well as Sharon Bajer's *Gingerbread Girl* and Ellen Peterson's *On the Shelf*, both currently under commission by PTE.

Before we get this show on the road, there are some thanks in order. We Playwrights Unit members are eternally grateful for the existence of PTE, Bob Metcalfe, and the Carol Shields Festival of New Works for giving us "leave to do our utmost."

Left to right: Actors Jennifer Lyon and Aaron Pridham, staged reading, The Carol Shields Festival of New Works.

We are also grateful to the people who have helped us put this collection together, especially the incredible and gracious Brian Drader, Executive Director of the Manitoba Association of Playwrights, who edited this anthology, and Karen Haughian of Scirocco Drama for taking on this project. Thank you as well to Michelle Lagassé, Festival Coordinator extraordinaire of the Carol Shields Festival of New Works, Tracey Loewen, PTE's General Manager, and Haanita Seval, PTE's Director of Marketing and Development, for contributing your knowledge and support.

And we are grateful to you, gentle reader, for your interest in new work and your willingness to climb into our collective brain for a while. It's an absurd, touching, sarcastic, and mostly comical place where anything can happen. We hope you enjoy.

Love,
The PTE Playwrights Unit

Fare Thee Well, Bob

When I first heard that Bob Metcalfe was appointed the new Artistic Director at Prairie Theatre Exchange 15 years ago, my first response was "He's got such a great wife!" I grew up in Vancouver and Bob and I attended the same theatre school, Studio 58 (although Bob graduated *waaayyyy* ahead of me). His beautiful wife Miriam Smith had been a prominent actress on Vancouver stages and I was so excited that she was coming to our community. She definitely eclipsed Bob's arrival, for me. On Bob's first day in Winnipeg we made him sit through a reading of my first full-length play, *Molly's Veil*, and I think he must have been jet-lagged because I do believe he slept through it. I may have imagined that. What I couldn't have imagined back then was how much of a champion Bob would be for us, and how much of a *brother* he would come to be for me.

One of his first questions was "Where are all the local playwrights?" We were here: writing in our homes, workshopping plays at the Manitoba Association of Playwrights, getting the odd production on local stages, or self-producing our work. Theatre Projects Manitoba was doing great work in developing and producing Manitoba playwrights, but our presence at PTE was never as fully supported as when Bob created the Playwrights Unit. The PU, The Unit, The PWU, the Group of Shame, the "Punit" (we've called it many things over the years) didn't include all of the playwrights in Manitoba, but our group has been together for over a decade. Some members have left or moved away, new members have joined, but it has continued to grow and evolve because of Bob's insight, guidance, support, good humour, and his endearing *love*, often disguised, but always felt.

Bob, we are dedicating this collection of Short Shots to you for everything you've done to support all of us in the Playwrights Unit. You have pitched our plays in other cities, given us amazing support from inception to full production, you have worked tirelessly writing grants, supporting our process, giving us feedback, workshopping and directing our plays, and genuinely believing in us as artists. Although we will probably miss Miriam and your children Laura and Maddy more, you will continue to be a part of us. And as you head to the cherry blossom, crocus-blooming-in-February city of Vancouver, we know that you will miss this frozen tundra that will always have a part of your heart.

Your loving *sister*,
Sharon Bajer

The Long & Short of It

The Chosen One
by Joseph Aragon

Late evening. The living room of a small house in a small, spartan town in rural Manitoba. Prominent Canadian author MARTHA Bostwick and her mother are arguing.

MA: I can show you where the probe went in!

MARTHA: Ma!

MA: If that's what it takes to get you to believe me.

MARTHA: Really, Ma, you don't need to…

MA: No, Martha. Look.

MA lifts up her sweater to reveal a small scar in her side.

MARTHA: …oh my God. Where did that come from?

MA: The probe!

MARTHA: C'mon, Ma, did you have a fall within the last few months? Jimmy told me you've been falling a lot lately.

MA: Jimmy's a damn liar! His kind always lies.

MARTHA: Ma, that's enough.

MA: Why is it that everything out of Jimmy's mouth is gold, but when your mother – *your own mother* is trying to tell you the truth –

MARTHA: That's enough!

MA: – you won't gimme the time of day?

MARTHA: Ma!

MA: You think I'm lying about this? You think I'm crazy?

MARTHA: I think –

MA: That's it, isn't it? I'm senile! Ma's finally off her rocker, gone seeing pretty lights in her head –

MARTHA: Ma, I'm not thinking that!

MA: Then what? What other reason do you have for not believing your own mother?!

MARTHA: Ma! – ...I think...I think you're just getting caught up in the craze.

MA: Oh for the love of –

MARTHA: Everybody is! My God, Ma, have you seen the front of Pete's store? Every news truck in the country's parked out there! They had the main strip lit up like Yankee Stadium, it was insane!

And I ran into Shirley this afternoon. She had her hair done. She never gets her hair done. She drove down to Winkler to get it done. She wants to look good for the cameras, she said. I'm telling you, the entire town's gone nuts.

MA: We know what we saw.

MARTHA: Do you? Really?

MA: We were all there, we saw it at the same time, we weren't hallucinating.

MARTHA: Jimmy didn't say anything about it.

MA: Because Jimmy was *not* there, so he did *not* see it, just like *you* weren't, so stop talking out your ass!

MARTHA: Are you sure it wasn't a plane?

MA: Planes don't hover.

MARTHA: A helicopter?

MA: Helicopters don't zigzag on a dime.

MARTHA: Maybe it's a top-secret military project.

MA: *Canadian* military?

MARTHA: All right.

MA: And they got a bunch of smart guys from NORAD or wherever saying the same thing. A blip on their radar or something. What would you say that was? Santa Claus?

MARTHA: That would be a lot more believable. Now Ma, really, where did that scar come from?

MA: The probe! –

MARTHA: Besides the goddamn probe!

Silence.

Well?

MA: There's no use talking to you anymore.

Silence. MARTHA looks out the window.

MARTHA: I see they got Shirley. She's yakking up a storm. At least they're not using the damn floodlights. When I talked to her this morning, she was excited about meeting Peter Mansbridge. I tried to tell her she probably wasn't going to, but no, she was absolutely convinced she was going to meet Peter Mansbridge tonight.

MA: Well. You know Shirley. She's an idiot.

MARTHA: I just wanna run right out there and yank her away. Save her from humiliating herself on national television.

MA: She's just telling her story, Martha. She may not be bright but she knows how to tell the truth. Besides, the rest of us had our turn, let her have her moment in the sun. Look how she's enjoying herself –

MARTHA: Wait – ...you talked to the media?

MA: Yeah, we all did.

MARTHA: What did you tell them?

MA: Well, I just told them about the lights in the sky, and how weird they were moving.

MARTHA: Was that it?

MA: Yeah.

MARTHA: Good.

MA: And, of course, I told them about my probe.

MARTHA: Oh, you didn't.

MA: They asked what happened, I told them what happened! It was on the night we first saw the lights. I tried to get to sleep as best I could, though given what I'd just seen, it was no easy task, believe you me. But I was just about to nod off when suddenly a bright light flooded my bedroom, and I felt myself being lifted off and carried out the window. Next thing I knew, I was on a cold metal table, with these creatures hovering over me. They looked like Nips.

MARTHA: Like what?

MA: Nips. You know. Nips?

MARTHA: I hope to God you didn't use that word on television.

MA: What word?

MARTHA: That word!

MA: What's wrong with –

MARTHA: You can't just go around saying that word!

MA: Why! We use it all the time, 'specially when we talk about Jimmy.

MARTHA: And Jimmy's not even Japanese! They don't know who you are, right?

MA: I gave them my name.

MARTHA: But they don't know who your daughter is? They don't know that Martha Bostwick is your daughter?

MA: Why should they? It's not even the same last name.

MARTHA: ...Good.

Silence.

MA: What's wrong with Boychuk? You couldn't have used Boychuk? It's not a hard name, it doesn't have five z's in a row like some Polack name.

Silence.

And "nip" is such a cute word! The puppy nipped at my heels! It's nippy outside! I'll have a nip with fries!

MARTHA: Ma!

Silence.

You know what, I'm just gonna go home tomorrow.

MA: But you can't!

MARTHA: You're fine, Ma! I flew here 'cause you said you were sick and you needed help but you're obviously fine! You're moving around okay, you got Shirley and the other girls looking out for you...you'll be fine.

MA: No, dear, you don't understand –

MARTHA: *(Consults Blackberry.)* If I leave early enough I could meet with my editor in the afternoon –

MA: Martha, listen! ... I was sick, but now I'm not.

MARTHA: Yes, obviously.

MA: But do you know why?

MARTHA: ...Why – ?

MA: The probe!! Listen. When you talked to Shirley and the others, did they say anything about me? About my health?

MARTHA: They said you had trouble getting around for a while.

MA: Oh, you don't know the half of it, missy. I was bedridden for a good three weeks.

MARTHA: What?

MA: Joints froze up and everything, like the Tin Man. Shirley had to wheel me around town. But then the lights in the sky came. And the probe. The probe did something to me. It cured me.

MARTHA: Ma –

MA: And there's something else too –

MARTHA: Ma, look, your rheumatism is –

MA: There's something else –

MARTHA: It's been cold here lately, right?

MA: Yeah.

MARTHA: But it began to warm up just when I got here. Right?

MA: There's something else, Martha!

MARTHA: ...Okay. What.

MA:	...I think they want to take me.
MARTHA:	Who.
MA:	The Nips!
MARTHA:	Ma!
MA:	You know who I'm talking about. They wanna take me.
MARTHA:	Where!
MA:	I dunno! Wherever it is they usually go. Andromeda. That's a planet, right?
MARTHA:	It's a galaxy.
MA:	Well, wherever it is, they wanna take me.
MARTHA:	How do you even know? Did they talk to you?
MA:	I just do. I think the probe's talking to me.
MARTHA:	But why? Why would they want to take you?
MA:	Why wouldn't they wanna take me?
MARTHA:	Yeah, but what makes you special?
MA:	Well, what makes *you* special?!
MARTHA:	Ma – ...I can't believe I'm arguing this...
	Usually...in the movies at least...when something like this happens, they choose someone special, someone who has a talent or a secret or the key to the survival of the universe or something. So... what are your qualifications?
MA:	...I dunno. I didn't know there was a rule you had to be "special." I just thought it was nice to be asked. Maybe they don't want special. Maybe they're looking for someone completely ordinary to represent Earth. I mean, if they brought home Albert Einstein, then they'd think everyone on Earth was like Albert Einstein, and that's not very accurate, is it – ?

MARTHA: You're not going anywhere! Shirley is not meeting Peter Mansbridge and you're not travelling to Andromeda! That's that!

MA: You just don't want me to, do you! Why don't you want this for me?

MARTHA: *You are not going to –*

MA: You've got your adventures, why can't I have mine? You're out east going to your book launches and your fancy rich galas, meanwhile I'm stuck here with bad rheumatism and nothing to do but keep Shirley company. And now these fellas come down and offer me the chance of a lifetime, to do something that no one else on Earth has ever done, and you say I can't 'cause I'm not special enough?

MARTHA: That's not what I –

MA: Well, lemme ask you again, missy, what makes *you* special? What is it you've done that makes you so damn fantastic?

MARTHA: What is it I've done? I dunno if you've noticed, Ma, but I've made a bit of a name for myself!

MA: Well la-di-da, miss princess, you sold a few books. So what.

MARTHA: One of them was nominated for a GG!

MA: Pff. *Nominated*.

MARTHA: What the hell do I have to do, turn water into wine?!

MA: Well, what the hell do *I* have to do?

Pause.

Seems like everyone's got something to prove. Otherwise they're nothing. "What can you give? What can you do?" Well, look at me, what *can* I do? But see, those fellas up there, they don't care. They just want Plain Old Me. And I'm gonna fly around in that thing and I'm gonna get to do stuff.

Pause.

I know I embarrass you, Martha, I'm not dumb. I know the town embarrasses you. Buncha nobodies in the middle of nowhere. But they landed *here*. They chose *me*.

Silence.

MARTHA: All right. I won't argue the matter.

MA: You still don't believe me.

MARTHA: Whether I believe you or not, you'll do what you think is best. If what you say is true, they'll whisk you away and you'll have a grand old time. Far be it from me to stand in the way.

MA: But are you happy for me?

MARTHA: Ma, I can't answer that –

MA: Okay, fine. *Would* you be happy for me?

MARTHA: …Well…depends. Are you happy for *me*?

Pause.

MA: …Yeah. Sure. I guess so. You seem to be doing well for yourself. I suppose having a book writer for a daughter is a pretty neat thing.

MARTHA: Then I suppose having an intergalactic explorer for a mother is a pretty neat thing too. I better pack.

MA: When do you think you'll be back to visit?

MARTHA: I dunno. When do you think *you'll* be back?

MARTHA leaves. MA is left alone in the room.

Suddenly, a blinding white light floods the room. MA rises from her chair, grabs her walker, and shuffles to the window, staring into the light.

End of Play.

Chess
by Sharon Bajer

SAM and LEO are playing chess. They are both five years old.

LEO: This is my brother's game.

SAM: Hey! My dad has this movie!

LEO: Chess?

SAM: No…um, he has the yellow guy movie.

LEO: Chess?

SAM: Yeah, chess.

LEO: Can you show me that? 'Cause I never watched it.

SAM: I don't have it, it's only for big guys. Only if you're adult. When you're adult…I'll show you.

LEO: Uhhhhh…when you were big, did you watch it?

SAM: No, um, it's a little bit scary. It will make you cry.

LEO: This guy has a sword.

SAM: I know. Okay, I'm…I'm gonna do this one.

LEO: You can only go die-nag-ally…doing the bombs.

SAM: Oooooooh.

LEO: On the next turn you can bomb this guy, but it's my turn, right?

SAM: Yeah.

LEO: *(He goes.)* Boom.

SAM: Now I'll bomb you!

LEO: But, okay, be very careful. Be very careful what you're doing, okay? Do you know why you have to be very careful?

SAM: Why, why?

LEO: Because the most important part...you have to look right here that I could bomb you back...so you have to...you have to watch out for that! Do you want to get your queen back?

SAM: Yeah.

LEO: Then on the next turn, move that guy there...and this guy will die. But you'll get your queen back! The queen is very powerful.

SAM: Why?

LEO: 'Cause she can go sideways, die-nag-ally and backwards...and frontwards and side to side. I'd call that powerful.

SAM: Yeah. It's my turn. Now I'm gonna do this guy. *(He goes.)* De, dun, dun, DUN!

LEO: Dead! And you get your queen back! Where was she?

SAM: She was right here.

LEO: No.

SAM: I think so.

LEO: WHERE WAS SHE?

SAM: I don't know! I thought she was right here.

Pause.

Leo picks up the queen and shakes it and puts it down again.

LEO: Is it my turn now?

SAM: Yeah.

LEO: So –

SAM: Actually it's my turn!

LEO: You already moved. Remember you did the bomb.

SAM: Oh yeah.

LEO: *(Moves.)* Dun dun da dun. Horses…those guys can only move in a L shape. That was a big L shape.

SAM: Yeah. *(Moves.)* Da da din din din.

LEO: No no no. Watch. Like this. Watch. Do do da doo din…but, but, if there's a red guy there you can do dun did a dun dun. You have to go like that. That's the L.

SAM: Yeah *(Moves.)* Dunh da dunh…da.

LEO: Good. Now, you already had your turn. MY TURN!

SAM: Yeah. And when I get bombed. I get to go in there.

LEO: Yeah.

SAM: Someone has to bomb me.

LEO: Well…move this guy.

Sam moves.

LEO: Oh my. Now you know what I'm gonna do?

SAM: What?

LEO: Boom. Now you're dead.

SAM: I got DEAD.

LEO: Yeah. Now you're DEAD. Now you go here.

SAM: Yeah. There.

LEO: This is my brother's game.

SAM: It's a fun game, right?

LEO: Mm hm. If somebody kills that the game's over. Hey, how did I kill that third one?

SAM: And you know what? These are the kids that… dead.

LEO: Yeah, they're DEAD.

SAM: Good.

LEO: Now…

SAM: Ah!

LEO: Avalanche is comin'!

SAM: What is "avalanche"?

LEO: Avalanche.

SAM: What does "avalanche" mean?

LEO: That means a big…BIG…one hundred billion million zero…thingin' boo…bibby bah…zero…one hundred, fifty below…bum bum…fee. And…and then snow comes pouring down…that much snow! And then it knocks down…and then…like…people die. An avalanche that's what it's called. And a avalanche…and a avalanche…and a avalanche…and a big…huge…avalanche!

Sam giggles.

(*Counting chess pieces.*) 1, 2, 3, 4, 1, 2, 3, 4.

SAM: That make…s eight! Watch! 1, 2 –

LEO: I know! I know! Eight! (*He covers his ears.*)

SAM: No! I count…I'm just counting…for…for…me.

LEO: Okay.

SAM: ….5, 6, 7, 8. I'm done.

They go back to the game.

LEO: You can only move die-nag-ally. The queen is blocking him and this guy's blocking him.

SAM: If that guy...kills my 'nother queen...I need to go back.

LEO: Uh oh. (*He knocks over the queen.*)

SAM: Queen down!

LEO: Two times! You wanna get your queen back, dontcha?

SAM: Yeah. But wait...this guy can go here and then I can get my queen back!

LEO: (*Doing a little dance.*) Oh no! My hands! Oh no! My hands! My hands!

SAM: I'mmmm....done playing this. (*Leo shrugs.*) Because you're not playing.

Pause.

Leo drops to the floor.

LEO: I'm playing.

SAM: So I moved that guy to...here.

LEO: (*Moving a piece.*) Dun da daaaa!

SAM: (*Moving a piece.*) Dun da daaaaa! Dee da da da da. Good. So, Unh, unh.

LEO: (*Moving a piece.*) Unh...or... unh.

SAM: Good. (*Moving a piece.*) Unh.

LEO: (*Starts dancing again.*) Everybody dance now.

They both start dancing and karate chopping the air with sound effects.

(*Returning to the game.*) C'mon!

SAM: (*Moving a piece.*) Ooooh.

LEO:	He can't kill forwards. He can only kill side to side.
SAM:	Now I'm going to use something eevil. I'm gonna use…this guy…to kill…this guy? I think? Or this guy…I mean this guy.
LEO:	NOOOOOOOO!!!!!
SAM:	Uh…I just didn't know.
LEO:	Do you want to kill this guy? Or that guy?

Sam knocks a piece over.

LEO:	Good. He's going to the hopistal. NEE NOO NEE NOO. AH! He got thrown to a grave when he was in the truck going to the hopistal. AHHHHH!
SAM:	Now…I'm gonna do something easily.
LEO:	Where you lookin'? Where you lookin'? *(Pause.)* Do you want the game over?
SAM:	*(Shakes his head no.)* This guy goes…
LEO:	He can't go die-nag-ally.

Pause.

SAM:	Straight?
LEO:	Yup.
SAM:	Now…I'm done.
LEO:	But then…then we have to stop playing.
SAM:	But I want to stop playing because I want to do that one. *(He points to another game.)*
LEO:	But I like this game.

Pause.

SAM:	*(Moving another piece.)* Din din din din…
LEO:	Want the game over now?

SAM: Yeah.

LEO: AVALANCHE!

They knock all the remaining pieces over.

End of Play.

Rage: A Love Story
by Rick Chafe

A restaurant. JULIE and WAYNE, a middle-aged married couple.

JULIE: Twenty years.

WAYNE: Pretty good.

JULIE: Not bad.

WAYNE: This is nice.

JULIE: Yeah. And we're doing…?

WAYNE: Made it through a meal.

JULIE: Just about. Congratulations.

WAYNE: To us.

They toast.

Pause.

JULIE: So Dave, across the lane. You know what he does today? He didn't actually let the cats into his house this time. He's leaving food out for them. I caught him. I held up my phone over the fence and I've got him on videotape putting food out for the cats. Proof.

WAYNE: Can we…? Just. We're almost through dinner. No talk about Dave and the cats.

JULIE: *(Beat.)* Okay. At work. They're bringing in a consultant. *Another* consultant –

WAYNE: Your work is off the table. We agreed.

JULIE: Yes. Sorry. You're right.

WAYNE: If you like, we could talk about my work?

JULIE: If you do, I will scream.

WAYNE: Don't want that. How about we just try to make it through dinner?

JULIE: One thing?

WAYNE: All ears.

JULIE: Well, if we're going to make another twenty years.

WAYNE: Yeah.

JULIE: Well. Something's gotta change.

WAYNE: Agreed.

JULIE: Before we make it one more year, for God's sake –

WAYNE: Agreed. Let's get through dessert, and *then* –

JULIE: *Before* dessert.

WAYNE: So like, five minutes.

JULIE: I want a new plan and a commitment before dessert.

WAYNE: Good luck.

JULIE: Or –

WAYNE: It's over.

JULIE: Yes.

WAYNE: Good. Suggestions?

A SERVER, in her 20s, enters.

SERVER: How are we doing? Can I offer you something sweet to finish with? Are you feeling kind of apple pie-ish? Or triple deluxe chocolate sex with Satan?

WAYNE:	Pie.
JULIE:	I'll have Satan.
SERVER:	And coffee?
WAYNE:	Decaf.
JULIE:	Double espresso.
SERVER:	I'll have that for you in five minutes.
	Exits.
WAYNE:	Five minutes. Go.
JULIE:	I don't know. You go. Are you going to contribute to this at all?
WAYNE:	You know my thoughts on the matter.
JULIE:	We're not doing a fucking nudist colony.
WAYNE:	Good. Ball's back to you.
JULIE:	You know where I stand.
WAYNE:	I'm not now or ever going on a reality show.
JULIE:	An entrenched position is not going to move us forward.
WAYNE:	You have 30 seconds. How would you even get us on to some stupid fucking reality show?
JULIE:	It doesn't matter! It's a quest! It's a joint venture to give us some kind of energy so we can move forward together instead of atrophying and calcifying. Just the act of planning something new and dreaming and applying ourselves and research and some hope! I am fifty and I want some focused target to keep my eye on instead of this downward spiral to death, yoked to your determination never to exist outside this single half acre of hell!
SERVER:	*(Entering.)* Um, hi. Could we just…down a notch? The other tables.

WAYNE: Not a problem.

SERVER: Sorry to mention it. Thanks! *(Exits.)*

WAYNE: Good. Done. Now stop. Off the table.

JULIE: You fear conflict.

WAYNE: I live with you.

JULIE: You aren't even offering alternatives.

WAYNE: I know.

JULIE: You're afraid of adventure, of anything new, you don't take responsibility for anything –

WAYNE: And you believe in fairies.

JULIE: That is completely out of context. And it's off the table.

WAYNE: You're right. I'm sorry.

JULIE: Around-the-world vacation.

WAYNE: Not a chance.

JULIE: Why not?

WAYNE: Next.

JULIE: If we could have had a child –

WAYNE: Stop. Why are you doing this? Why are you even going there? That is so completely off the table.

JULIE: Yes. And I will not go there. That is why we sell everything. Every single thing. One sale price. Half a million takes the house, the car, everything in it. We could get that easy. We go to Africa and start an orphanage.

WAYNE: Are you just trying to piss me off?

JULIE: I am trying to squeeze a single drop of blood from the rock of Gibraltar.

WAYNE: Not before dessert. Not tonight at all. In the morning, I promise, I'll be open to anything.

JULIE: Build the addition.

WAYNE: No.

JULIE: The bathroom.

WAYNE: Not doing the bathroom again.

JULIE: A rec room.

WAYNE: You don't need a rec room.

JULIE: Then it's the kitchen.

WAYNE: I'm not spending another twenty years tearing apart the whole house over and over again just to give you something to get excited about.

JULIE: One tiny dream, is all I'm asking, for *us* to get excited about.

WAYNE: Have your dream. Just don't inflict it on me.

JULIE: That's what couples do.

WAYNE: Inflict themselves on each other.

JULIE: Yes. It's called love. Two lives joining together. Sharing and caring.

WAYNE: What would you know about that?

JULIE: Quite a bit more than you, you self-centred, self-satisfied, supercilious prick.

WAYNE: That's enough.

JULIE: No. Tell me. Right now. What in hell is going to get us through another twenty years? Why do we keep going? Why should we? Why should I even stay? We barely got through the first twenty, there is no reason for us to be together another day unless something changes, so what is it going to be? What are you going to put on the table?

WAYNE: I'm too angry to even have this discussion, and so are you. I will talk about it. But in the morning when we've calmed down.

JULIE: No. Before that dessert gets here or forget it. Twenty years is enough. Give me something now or when I get home I'm calling a taxi and getting out of your life forever.

Pause.

WAYNE: All right. The kitchen.

JULIE: I mean it.

WAYNE: Don't you dare question me. You are on thin fucking ice! I said I will renovate the kitchen. If it takes a year – and shut up about contractors –

SERVER: *(Entering.)* Please, sir –

WAYNE: Right!

SERVER exits.

(Quietly furious.) We're not hiring anyone, I'm doing this myself because I want to be able to retire one day and this is going to cost us half the mortgage to put in your extension and foundation and your gas appliances and your granite counters so yes, I will take a year of my time and my life, all my evenings, all my weekends. But don't question me.

JULIE: All right. You're right.

WAYNE: Have I ever failed to do something I promised?

JULIE: No. You haven't.

WAYNE: Have I ever not come through on something I said I would do for you?

JULIE: No. You're the best.

WAYNE: Have I ever betrayed you, screwed around on you, lied to you, been anything but good to you other than my obvious and many faults and shortcomings and inadequacies?

JULIE: No. You're right. This is good.

WAYNE: And now ask yourself. Why am I going to drive myself to the outer limits of my abilities? Though it will cost me my skin which will flay from my body, and my blood that will seep out through my wounds, my fingernails that crack and split and pull away at the roots, my nerves that dry and stretch and crack, and the discs in my back that pop and bulge and herniate. I will do this. Just to get you off my back. And what am I getting in return? What's your piece in this? Anything? What are you going to contribute? What is this going to cost you? *(By now, very loud.)* What could you possibly give that will make all this worth anything for me? Because a year from now, when you have a kitchen, I will be all used up. Unless you bring something, something to the table. You tell me what that is. *You* tell *me* what that is right now. Or you can get in that taxi with my blessing.

JULIE: I don't know.

WAYNE: You what?

JULIE: I don't...

SERVER: *(Entering.)* I'm sorry, I'm afraid the manager has asked me to tell you both to leave.

WAYNE: He what?

SERVER: To leave. We have had every table in the restaurant complain about you now.

WAYNE: Every table.

SERVER: Every table.

JULIE: Well. Every table. Then it's unanimous.

SERVER: Please. I am very sorry.

JULIE: You little pissy-assed fuck.

SERVER: Please. We really don't want any more of a scene.

JULIE: This is my husband. This is the man I love. We have been married twenty years. And he has just proclaimed his love for me on this very day. And he did not do it politely, he did not do it quietly, and there's a reason for that, which you would not understand, you little shit, because you are only concerned about making your tips for the night –

SERVER: Actually, it was the manager who asked –

JULIE: The manager, not even the owner, someone hired to protect the mediocreness of this mediocrity of a really not very good restaurant so that this *clientele* can gather and pretend that they are so important that they can be protected from the realities of life by their toothless ass-suck lapdog for hire, fuck! Well, we're not going to stand in the way of you doing your job. My husband and I are going to go home with our 50-year-old bodies and do something even more disgusting, we're going to have gross, wrinkly, saggy, 50-year-old sex!

SERVER: Good. Lovely. Enjoy yourselves.

JULIE: Oh, we will! You puke!

SERVER: Thank you. Good night.

They step away from the table. The SERVER exits. They might be outside now.

WAYNE: I had this vision just then. You were fifteen years old again.

JULIE: We never knew each other when we were fifteen.

WAYNE: You were fifteen. I was seventeen. And the world seemed very sad. And the wind blew. And it was cold. But I had my hand wrapped around yours. And damn them all, I knew I could do anything.

They exit, hand in hand.

End of Play.

The Propeller Moment
by Ginny Collins

JEFF, in his mid-fifties, and ANNE, forties or fifties, are on a film set, in the director's tent, sitting in front of a monitor. JEFF is in his director's chair. His soul is tired. ANNE, the producer, is wearing a headset, watching the monitor carefully.

ANNE: Ok, it's coming up…oh, not yet, we pan to the barn first, hang on.

ANNE watches the monitor intently. JEFF yawns and checks his watch.

Wait for it…Oh! It's coming, watch…there! See what she's doing there?

ANNE looks for a response that does not come.

It's strange, right?

JEFF: I don't know what you're talking about.

ANNE: She's a zombie. She's about to be killed. Why is she doing that?

JEFF: What!?

ANNE: That! That thing with her hands. What is that?

JEFF: How should I know?

ANNE: Well, what did you direct her to do?

JEFF: I didn't direct her at all.

ANNE: Well, that's not how zombies act in real life.

JEFF: Isn't it?

ANNE: Jeff, I'm not telling you how to do your job –

JEFF: Uh huh.

ANNE: – but we need to do another take. She can't be doing that.

JEFF: We don't need to do another take.

ANNE: Maybe we need to watch it again.

ANNE reaches for the monitor.

JEFF: No, no. Anne, listen, I know what I'm doing. It's my job to take care of this stuff. It's your job to nag everybody about money.

ANNE: That's not –

JEFF: Yes it is. "Time is money." That's your line. All I'm doing is keeping us on budget. I've done 39 of these. Sequels, slashers, you name it. And if I've learned anything, it's that details don't matter. People don't watch these movies to like them. They don't care about actor choices or fuckin' irregular zombie behaviour. They want to get turned on and grossed out. End of story.

ANNE: So you don't care at all about this movie.

JEFF: Anne! I care deeply about this movie, alright? This is my last film. It will make me just enough money to retire comfortably and never ever have to talk to another producer again, no offence.

ANNE: Ya.

JEFF: I am happy to disappear into obscurity so if anyone asks what I did for a living, I can tell them I was a real estate agent.

ANNE: That's awful.

JEFF: I have come to terms with the fact that I will never create anything memorable, or even good. That way I don't have to try. It's freeing. I recommend it.

ANNE: So it's about the paycheque.

JEFF: Now you're learning.

ANNE: Well, that paycheque won't exist if I can't sell this film. And I won't sell this film if the zombies aren't acting like zombies. When people buy a zombie movie, there are expectations.

JEFF: Right. Well, you know what? Why don't we worry about this tomorrow. Everyone is tired, we should –

ANNE: (*Into her headset.*) Send the girl zombie in here, please.

JEFF: C'mon!

ANNE: We'll do this fast.

ZOMBIE actor, female, late twenties, enters. She is grotesque, with multiple wounds and one dangling eyeball.

ZOMBIE: You wanted to see me?

ANNE: Yes.

Pause. They all wait.

ANNE pokes JEFF.

JEFF: Oh! Yes. That thing you're doing, please stop doing it.

ZOMBIE: What thing?

Pause.

JEFF: What thing?

ANNE: That thing you're doing with your hands, when the lead character is about to kill you. When you clasp your hands together. Just don't do that. Just die like a zombie would die. That's all.

ZOMBIE: Oh.

ANNE: Do you understand?

ZOMBIE: Um…yes…

ANNE: Is there a problem?

ZOMBIE: No. I just…I did have a reason.

JEFF: (*Rubs his face.*) Oh, here we go.

ANNE: A reason?

ZOMBIE: Well, my character is attacked by zombies when she's in church, right? She's obviously very pious. So when she's turned into a zombie she loses her soul, which would be devastating for a religious person. I was thinking that when my character's zombie got killed she's essentially dying again, right? She's having a second death. It's deep. So she would have this glimmer of realization and mourning for the fact that her soul will never ascend to heaven like she's always wanted. When I clasped my hands together like that, it was my character offering a final prayer for her soul.

    Pause.

ANNE: You're kidding.

ZOMBIE: Ummm…

ANNE: Your character's name is Girl in Church. You have two lines. This is not your story. Please do as you've been told. We don't have time for this.

ZOMBIE: What does he think? (*Points to JEFF.*)

ANNE: Him?

ZOMBIE: He's the director.

ANNE: He thinks you should act like a zombie.

ZOMBIE: Do you think that?

JEFF grunts.

ZOMBIE: Hey, I'm not fooling myself. I know we're making a shitty movie here. I just thought we could create a "moment."

JEFF laughs.

ANNE: Ok –

ZOMBIE: I'm just stating my case.

ANNE: We're done here.

ANNE takes her arm and begins to escort her out.

JEFF: Hey! Careful! Unions!

ANNE lets go and ZOMBIE approaches the director.

ZOMBIE: Don't you want a propeller moment?

JEFF: A what?

ANNE: I'm calling security.

JEFF: (*To ANNE.*) It's fine. (*To ZOMBIE.*) What's a propeller moment?

ZOMBIE: It's that moment in a movie that everyone remembers. That you can't ever get out of your head and you're not sure why.

ANNE: She's wasting our time.

JEFF: Go on.

ZOMBIE: In the movie *Titanic*, there's one moment in the movie that everyone who's ever seen it remembers. When we watched it we all felt the same thing. You know what it is.

JEFF: When the boat sinks?

ANNE: The boat sinks for two hours!

ZOMBIE: It's near the end. When the *Titanic* is standing vertically like this. The people who made it to the front of the ship are hanging on, their feet dangling. Then this one guy falls off and he –

JEFF: Hits the propeller!

ZOMBIE: Exactly!

JEFF: That part is crazy! Do you remember that, Anne? He, like, spins out. Everybody's like "oooooh!"

ZOMBIE: It's what I call the propeller moment. It's a moment that sticks with you, even if the rest doesn't.

JEFF: Ok, but we're not exactly making *The Titanic* here, kid.

ZOMBIE: It doesn't matter. That moment wasn't about big-budget special effects. It was a mannequin hitting metal, but it was brave and considered and had just a bit of truth in it, y'know? You're watching it and you're like, "yeah, with all those people falling, somebody would have totally dinged the propeller on the way down. And it would have been just like that."

ANNE: Now can I start nagging about money?

ZOMBIE: These moments are everywhere. You can be reading the most mediocre book and then this one line of description will just jump out at you and knock you flat and you'll remember it your entire life. Or you'll be looking at a painter's shitty work but just one expression he's painted haunts you for some reason, but you can't quite put your finger on it. It's this unforgettable moment in an overall forgettable artistic experience. I want to be part of that.

ANNE:	Well, you're not.
JEFF:	Kid, I'll be honest with you, I really don't think we have one of those propeller moments on our hands here.
ANNE:	Jeff, we need to end this.
ZOMBIE:	But you don't know that. You'll never make one if you never try.
JEFF:	Zombies die every day. It's nothing special.
ZOMBIE:	And that's what everyone will be expecting. Nothing special. That's when you hit them. You make them feel when they least expect it. Get 'em in the gut. They'll remember.
ANNE:	(*Begins dialing on her cell phone.*) You're being replaced.
JEFF:	It'll never work.
ANNE:	Jeff, the girl from the coffee shop scene looks enough like her. With makeup we can –
JEFF:	The hand clasping doesn't read clearly enough. We'll have you fall to your knees, keep the hands clasped, and I want you to look into your killer's eyes and that look should have all the fear of a soul that knows it's damned.
ANNE:	No!
ZOMBIE:	Yes!
JEFF:	Can you do that?
ZOMBIE:	I sure can.
JEFF:	Alright, go.
	ZOMBIE *actor leaves the tent.* ANNE *glares at* JEFF.
ANNE:	This movie is going to be absolute shit.

JEFF: I know.

ANNE: She just conned you into giving her more screen time.

JEFF: I know.

ANNE: So why are you indulging this?

JEFF: You're telling me you don't remember that guy hitting the propeller? The way his body spins afterward? The sound it makes?

ANNE: So what's the point?

JEFF: The point is you remembered it. Someone created something that people remember.

Pause.

JEFF: Plus she was never gonna shut up.

ANNE: Ya, fair enough.

JEFF: (*Shouts.*) Quiet on set!

End of Play.

Life of Pie
by Trish Cooper

Three old friends, NIKKI, KATHRYN, and LISA have gathered at Lisa's family cottage with Lisa's mother GRACE.

KATHRYN enters to hear them all laughing. She joins in and tries to figure out what they are laughing about, which just makes them laugh harder.

KATHRYN: What did I miss? What's so funny?

They laugh some more.

GRACE: All settled? Did you get a drink? What can I get you? Beer, wine, ice-tea? Is it warm enough in your room? We'll put the heater on for a while when you're ready for bed.

KATHRYN: Oh, thank you, Grace, I have one started over here. Thanks again for having me. The cottage looks beautiful. I'm just so happy to be here.

GRACE: I can't remember the last time you were here, was it you last summer? We took out that wall and it really opens up this room.

More laughing.

KATHRYN: Seriously, what is so funny?

LISA: Oh, we were just trying to figure out where you bought the pies.

KATHRYN: What? I made the pies. I told you.

NIKKI: Oh right, you made them yourself. Nice job. They look lovely.

LISA: Yes, they look very homemade. Homemade pie by Kathryn.

NIKKI: I can't wait to try your pie!

LISA: What kind did you make, Kathryn? *(Laughing.)*

KATHRYN: Blueberry and uh, apple.

LISA: You don't remember.

KATHRYN: Oh. Is that the joke? You don't think I made these pies myself? Is that what's so hilarious?

NIKKI: I'm sure you made them yourself. Absolutely!

LISA: Did you use fresh ingredients from your garden?

KATHRYN: Yeah, fresh from my apple tree and my blueberry bush.

GRACE: Oh, go on.

KATHRYN: I'm joking. I bought groceries at Safeway and then I made the pies.

LISA: Oh, really. How did you get the crust so flakey?

KATHRYN: I bought the crusts.

They all start laughing again.

I didn't say I didn't buy the crusts. I'm not bragging. It wasn't a big deal but uh, I bought the crusts and then I put the fruit in them and I baked them.

NIKKI: Stella's or Gunn's?

LISA: Or Baked Expectations?

NIKKI: Sobeys bakery?

KATHRYN: I made the pie. I make pie.

LISA: She makes pie.

NIKKI: You're a pie maker now.

LISA: That's your thing. You're the pie person now. You make pies.

KATHRYN: Yeah, I guess it's been a while since I've seen you guys. I make pies. I make mushroom pies. Like roast vegetables in a pie. It's not hard. I just buy the crust and, it's not complicated.

NIKKI: I'm looking forward to tasting your pie.

LISA: What else goes in the pie with the fruit?

KATHRYN: Ok, whatever. I don't care what you guys think, let's just have a drink.

NIKKI: But I want to know, what else besides the apples? Do you follow a recipe?

KATHRYN's starting to lose her patience.

KATHRYN: No, it's just a little cinnamon, a bit of sugar and –

NIKKI: Sugar?

KATHRYN: It doesn't really need sugar, but –

NIKKI: No sugar?

KATHRYN: Why don't we drop the whole pie thing. I think you know I made the pie and you're just trying to fuck with me.

GRACE: Girls, just let it go. Let her think you believe her.

KATHRYN: It's fine, Grace. I don't care. I'm not going to get sucked into this.

LISA: Yeah, let's just enjoy the night. God, how long has it been?

KATHRYN: How's the new job, Nikki?

NIKKI: So far, it's great, but soon I think they will expect me to do something.

GRACE: Ladies, I made this gin lemonade drink. Anyone?

LISA: Thanks, Mom!

NIKKI: Perfect!

KATHRYN: Thanks, Grace. Sounds great!

GRACE pours the drinks.

LISA: Ladies! Back together again!

They all cheer.

KATHRYN: Cheers.

NIKKI: Cheers.

GRACE: Pleasure to have you here.

LISA: To old friends, new jobs and homemade pies.

Everyone laughs hysterically except KATHRYN.

Two hours later. Dinner has been eaten, plates have been cleared, and drinks have been replenished.

KATHRYN: Oh my god, you guys, I have to tell you. I don't think I told you about Christine Haniford.

NIKKI: Oh yeah, her and her husband split.

LISA: She's never looked better. She's dating a woman now.

KATHRYN: I know, I ran into her and –

LISA: She seriously looks so freaking good.

KATHRYN: I know, I'm at the Y and she comes up.

NIKKI: Her girlfriend is like a corporate millionaire or something.

KATHRYN: Nice, well, she –

GRACE: She really cleaned herself up. She must have been so depressed before. I never understood what she was doing with that David. He was just kind of a creep.

KATHRYN: So I'm at the Y and she comes up to me and I'm like "Hey Christine! You look great."

LISA: She looks great.

KATHRYN: So she says I don't go by Christine anymore. My name is AJ.

GRACE: AJ?

LISA: AJ?

KATHRYN: AJ.

NIKKI: She changed her name.

KATHRYN: I'm trying to tell the story.

NIKKI: So stupid, AJ? AJ!

KATHRYN: Don't yell at me. I'm just telling you what she said. And I said, Hmm. Do you mind if I ask why AJ?

LISA: Christine Haniford.

NIKKI: Christine Leslie Haniford. What the fuck? There is no AJ in any of her initials.

KATHRYN: I know, but she said…

LISA: God, I hate people with stupid names. Or people who change their names to something stupid. Or nicknames that make no sense.

KATHRYN: She said, I do mind, actually.

LISA: She minds what.

NIKKI: She asked if she minds.

GRACE: Minds what?

NIKKI: If she asks why AJ?

KATHRYN: She wouldn't tell me but her girlfriend told me. It's the initials for her spirit name.

LISA: You're lying.

GRACE: Her spirit name.

NIKKI: Isn't the whole point of a spirit name to be like dreaming bear or dancing frog or like a quality that someone has, like Healing Woman? You don't get a spirit name like AJ.

KATHRYN: The initials must stand for something

LISA: What do you know about spirit names? Busy with your spirit names?

NIKKI: Well, I'm so happy for AJ she looks so good and she's got this great lady and cheers to AJ.

They cheer to AJ.

LISA: Let's throw another log on this fire.

NIKKI: Does anyone want another beer?

They all get another drink.

KATHRYN: Is everyone full or anyone ready for some dessert?

They all burst out laughing.

LISA: You are really going to stick to this pie thing.

GRACE: Come on. Leave it alone. Why do you care? You didn't make that salsa from scratch.

LISA: I didn't say I made it from scratch. I bought it.

KATHRYN: I didn't say I made them from scratch either. I bought the crusts, and then I made the pie.

NIKKI: Honey, shhhh. Why are you freaking out about pie?

LISA: It's just pie.

GRACE: Girls, let's not fight over pie.

KATHRYN: I'm not mad about the pie. I don't care. I'm just going to take my pie and give it to someone who cares about me and my pie and my feelings.

NIKKI: Oh, settle down!

KATHRYN: And the thing that's really insane is, that I can't tell if you guys really seriously think I didn't make those pies, or if you believe me but are purposely trying to make me mad about you *pretending* about the pie. And either option is not good. Either way, it basically means that you are mean. You're mean, and like I'm going to bed soon and you guys can suck it.

LISA: Kathryn, don't get all upset.

KATHRYN: Like, have you ever known me to be a fake person that would lie about fake pie? Do we have that kind of friendship? We don't bullshit each other about our lives, and pretend we're happy when we're not. We don't dress nice for each other or pretend we have more money than we really have. I feel like this whole pie thing is just a sad turning point. Does this mean we start lying to each other and act fake and hide our feelings and are we going to stop trusting each other? Are we going to stop being real with each other? Like this whole pie thing is making me think that you two are a couple of bitches...not you, Grace, I love you, you're like a second mother to me and... I need you to believe me... I need you to know, I swear on my mother's grave, I baked these pies. I made them for all of us to enjoy, not to divide us, but to unite us. And I brought some vanilla ice cream...because we all enjoy vanilla.

Okay, I'm getting emotional ... I made the pie with my own hands. I made the pie.

LISA hugs KATHRYN.

LISA: Oh honey, oh no. Sweetie. I love you.

NIKKI: Okay, okay, it's okay.

GRACE: Maybe we should eat that pie before we get too drunk. I'll get some plates out.

LISA: Wow, this whole thing got a little ridiculous. Out of control. I'll get the ice cream.

KATHRYN: I guess I'm a little emotional.

NIKKI: Don't let Lisa get to you. She's just teasing you.

KATHRYN: I just don't think it's funny.

NIKKI: It went too far.

KATHRYN: You know I made that pie, right?

NIKKI: Oh my god.

KATHRYN: I know, I know, I'm being insane but seriously.

NIKKI: Let's talk about something else!

Pause. KATHRYN whispers.

KATHRYN: You believe me about the pie? Right? You know I made the pie.

NIKKI: *(Whispering back.)* I don't believe you. I don't believe that you made the pie.

End of Play

Preparing for Field Day
by James Durham

A MAN and a WOMAN sit opposite each other at a desk. There are several papers and books and files and note pads. The MAN is dressed in a tracksuit. The WOMAN is dressed in somewhat formal attire, a skirt and a business jacket. We catch her in mid sentence reading from a paper.

WOMAN: – and we are having the long jump, but it will be called just…jumping, the sprint will be called fun run, and we will have the "three legged race," but it will be called the "three legged dance." The entire theme of this so-called "Field Day" is about participating and being inclusive…there is no race…no competition –

MAN: – how do you know who wins –

WOMAN: – you don't need to know –

MAN: – I'm sorry, I mean, who wins the particular event –

WOMAN: – winning is irrelevant, "participating" is enough –

MAN: – winning defines the result of the event, ribbons are handed out, 1st, 2nd –

WOMAN: – we haven't done that for years –

MAN: – I'd like to reinstate it –

WOMAN:	– I'm sure there are people who would like to bring back segregation, but I think we have made progress, don't you?
MAN:	That's hardly ana…the same –
WOMAN:	Analogous? –
MAN:	– thing. Yes. Look, in sport there are clear winners…and people who are –
WOMAN:	– losers, my point –
MAN:	– not victorious –
WOMAN:	– exactly! Why are you so obsessed with who wins?
MAN:	I'm not –
WOMAN:	You seem to be –
MAN:	– it's about the nature of sport. We are having Field Day –
WOMAN:	"Participation Day"
MAN:	What?
WOMAN:	That's the appropriate nomenclature. *(She waves the paper at him.)* That's what I was getting to –
MAN:	What? Look, we are having athletic events and we are awarding –
WOMAN:	– the reward is intrinsic –
MAN:	How can we have Field Day or Participation Day without any incentive?
WOMAN:	The incentive is built in…the grace of the activity.

Pause.

MAN:	How does the three-legged dance work? They just tie a leg together and do what? Dance to the finish line?

Preparing for Field Day by James Durham

WOMAN:	There is no finish line, there is a reward line –
MAN:	What's the reward?
WOMAN:	Finishing, of course! Everyone will finish.

Pause.

MAN:	What's the point of all this –
WOMAN:	To include the kids who feel excluded; they are usually less aggressive and so are naturally prone to withdraw –
MAN:	Maybe it's our job to draw them out –
WOMAN:	We will if we proceed with my proposals. You don't seem to understand. There is intimidation in competition. We are trying to build self-esteem. We are trying to prepare them for the world, which is a very intimidating place.
MAN:	Exactly, so why aren't we preparing them for that kind of intimidation?
WOMAN:	This will. This also benefits in not only shaping them to meet the world, but we are also shaping them to be the kind of citizens we want.
MAN:	I agree that we are trying to give them self-esteem and prepare them for, etc., but there is a lot to learn from winning and losing, a great deal of maturing and learning happens after the result, you have to learn how to win and lose with dignity and grace.
WOMAN:	No –
MAN:	Yes –
WOMAN:	No, our job is to enable everyone to have a positive experience.
MAN:	Everyone can compete –
WOMAN:	Some won't –
MAN:	Then they need encouragement –

WOMAN: They won't because they already feel like a "loser."

Pause.

MAN: I oppose this.

WOMAN: That's obvious.

MAN: Would you like to hear my reasoning?

WOMAN: Your reasoning will negate the emotional needs of our students.

MAN: I haven't said anything yet –

WOMAN: Yes, you have. You have been "opposing," dare I say "fighting" with me, "competing" against my proposal in an attempt to "win" your argument to maintain the "blood sport" of your field day –

MAN: Blood sport!

WOMAN: All sport is a metaphor for war. I did a paper on it in my undergrad.

MAN: Okay. How did you look at winning and losing?

WOMAN: To make sport less violent and end cheating we have to eliminate winning and losing.

MAN: People wouldn't watch it.

WOMAN: I don't think men are watching women's beach volleyball to see who wins.

MAN: We're getting off topic –

WOMAN: You asked the question –

MAN: But that would kill sport, what about 'the thrill of victory and the agony of defeat' –

WOMAN: Exactly, there is nothing to be gained by elevating one student at the expense of another student's agony. It's abusive.

MAN:	That's not what I meant, I was talking about the spirit of competition –
WOMAN:	That's what you said. I'm merely responding to your statements –
MAN:	Let me try again, okay, look, we have eliminated so much, in the early years of our education system, about success and failure, in terms of grading, or even suggesting that the student has failed –
WOMAN:	No student fails! They "develop" at a different rate –
MAN:	But that's where sport differs –
WOMAN:	Which is why we have to change it –
MAN:	But we have to prepare them for the real world –
WOMAN:	We have to make a better world –
MAN:	You and I are in the real world –
WOMAN:	Yes –
MAN:	And we're arguing to win, are we not?
WOMAN:	No. We are having a discussion. Your patriarchal perception is unfortunately your problem, not mine.
MAN:	Don't patronize me. *(He pronounces it paytronize.)*
WOMAN:	It's *pat*ronize.

Pause.

MAN:	I'm screwed, aren't I?
WOMAN:	Why must you invoke a Victorian slang for coitus? It's a derogatory term which is really indicative of the rape culture that exists in sport today.
MAN:	Vajayjay!
WOMAN:	What? What are you calling me –

MAN: A big VAJAYJAY!

WOMAN: Name calling, well then, you have proven everything I have said.

Pause.

MAN: What am I gonna do?

WOMAN: Is that slang for vagina?

MAN: Yes –

WOMAN: Whatever you do, don't call her a Vajajay, that would be really stupid, and make you look equally pathetic. You would be…the bigger Vayjayjay.

MAN: I'm so frustrated.

WOMAN: Welcome to my world –

MAN: At least your world functions with reason.

WOMAN: Not so, there is a great deal of appealing to the emotions in the court, to the jury, even judge, why do you think we call him "your honour"? How you respect the judge is worth…two points if we're talking basketball. He might just let a little thing go in your favour. My suggestion is: not to get adversarial. I baited you and you ran with it. This is part of the preparation, you can't let your emotions get the better of you. Talk about the great women in sport that the young girls need to aspire to, talk about your love for sport –

MAN: Winning and losing is an experience you gain from, you can gain positively or negatively from either outcome. To negate the outcome, you offer no genuine learning experience. If you knock off the bar in the high jump, you've failed in your attempt. This lets you know that you have to try again. They want to remove the bar and have a teacher stand there and say "you made it." What's the point of trying to teach them the proper technique? Ah, screw it!

WOMAN: You're a great teacher. This is important, we live in an adversarial world. Whether we like it or not, "the bar is set." Our legal system is based on it. Being a defence attorney, it doesn't matter to me if my client is guilty or innocent, I'm there to serve my client's interests. Take for instance this rapist I'm defending –

MAN: He's guilty –

WOMAN: Looking at the evidence, yes, but I'm not the judge and jury, it's the Crown's job to win the conviction, it's the jury's job to convict if the evidence is convincing, it's the judge's job to make sure the procedure is followed. If they can't do the job then the law, the system is failing and we all lose. If I don't do my job then I don't test the system, and then we all lose. Trust me, it's no Field Day. Oh, you can say patronize either way. It's just British pronunciation versus American.

MAN: Thanks.

WOMAN: I hope you win.

MAN: I hope you lose.

End of Play.

The Routine
by Jason Neufeld

DON is lying in bed reading a book by nightlight. Offstage we hear rustling and a loud "thump."

DON: What are you doing in there?

DAWN: Nothing.

DON: Doesn't sound like nothing.

DAWN: Don't worry about it.

DON: You're gonna wake the neighbours.

DAWN: Just read your Archies.

DON does just that. After a short time, another "thump" is heard offstage.

DON: Seriously, Dawn, what are you doing?

DAWN slinks over to DON, who has put his Archie comic down, but hasn't made a move.

DAWN: What do you think?

DON: What's all this?

DAWN: What do you mean?

DON: First you didn't want to watch *Law and Order* and now this.

DAWN: It was a repeat.

DON: That's never stopped us before.

> *DAWN crawls onto the bed and throws the Archie comic across the room and it knocks over a bouquet of bamboo. Water and rocks spill onto the floor.*

Honestly, what has gotten into you?

> *DON goes to clean up the bamboo.*

DAWN: Just leave it!

DON: We can't just leave it. The water's going to seep into the floorboards. It'll just take a second. In the meantime you can tell me what's gotten into you.

DAWN: Do I seriously have to explain this?

DON: Yes.

DAWN: I have to explain walking into my bedroom with sexy lingerie.

DON: When it's a Monday night and I have to work the next day, yes, you do.

DAWN: You know what, Don, you suck!

DON: Careful! You're going to wake up the neighbours.

DAWN: Oh, you'd like that, wouldn't you!

DON: Keep your voice down.

DAWN: Don't shush me!

DON: Let's not make a scene tonight, okay?

DAWN: You think I'm ugly, don't you. You hate me.

DON: No, I don't think you're ugly.

DAWN: You think I'm ugly. I see the way you look at our neighbour. You don't look at me that way.

DON: You're crazy.

DAWN: You flirt with her right in front of me.

DON: I do not.

DAWN: You carried her groceries up to her apartment last week.

DON: So?

DAWN: So, you made me carry ours. We had four litres of milk in that bag.

DON: You're overreacting.

DAWN: Oh, am I? I've seen the way you look at her. You get this ridiculous grin on your face.

DON: I'm just being friendly. I'm being a good neighbour. I can't help it if I've got good manners, unlike some people I know.

DAWN: Let's not turn this around – we're not talking about me, we're talking about you and your lust for our eighteen-year-old neighbour.

DON: Stop this, you're embarrassing yourself.

DAWN: Oh, I haven't even begun to embarrass myself!

DON: Listen to yourself, you need to calm down.

DAWN: Is that what you want – a tight little rump?

DON: Stop it.

DAWN: Come to think of it, she kind of looks like Veronica, doesn't she?

DON: Don't be ridiculous.

DAWN: You're fantasizing about our neighbour because she reminds you of a character in a comic book.

DON: That's stupid.

DAWN: Sorry to burst your bubble, Jughead, but girls like that don't look that way forever. They get ugly and fat just like the rest of us.

DON: First of all, Jughead doesn't even like girls – look, can we not talk about this right now?

DAWN: Oh we'll talk, Donny boy, we'll talk. Your wife of seven years throws herself at you, and you can't be bothered? We'll talk.

DON: I'm just not in the mood. It's Monday night.

DAWN: You can't stand to look at me.

DON: That's not true.

DAWN: Yes, it is. You think I'm ugly and fat – and old.

DON: Well you *are* getting older, Dawn, we all are.

Pause.

DON: What?

DAWN: Why do you always have to be that way?

DON: What way?

DAWN: Why is it so hard to say, "Dawn, you're beautiful, and you look as young as the day I met you"?

DON: But you are older. So am I. I've got no problem with it. What's the big deal?

DAWN: The big deal is I think it's a big deal, and so it should be a big deal to you.

DON: So you want me to lie?

DAWN: No, I don't want you to lie. I want you to tell me I'm beautiful.

DON: Well, if I tell you you're beautiful now, it's not gonna count, is it? I mean, it's got to be spontaneous, or it just sounds like I'm faking it.

DAWN: Why don't you just try to see?

DON: This is ridiculous.

DAWN: Say it!

DON:	You're beautiful.
DAWN:	Liar!
DON:	What do you want from me?
DAWN:	The truth!
DON:	You're not making any sense. You need to calm down. Maybe you should take your Lorazepam.
DAWN:	You'd like that, wouldn't you?

DON gets up to get the pills.

Get back here, we're not done yet!

DON comes back into the room with a bottle of pills and shakes them at her.

Don't you shake those pills at me.

He shakes them again.

Give them to me.

DAWN lunges at DON and he hides the bottle behind his back. They struggle until they have fallen onto the bed together in a compromising position. He is underneath her and can't move. She has him pinned.

DON: You know, maybe you are a bit fatter.

No response.

I'm just saying, maybe a few more hours at the gym wouldn't hurt. You're always saying you want to get out of the house more – here's your chance.

No response.

Look, you asked me if I thought you were fat. I'm telling you the truth. I just want to support you if you want to get healthier.

DAWN: You're not playing fair.

DON: Look, you wanted the truth – I'm just giving you what you want.

No response.

Aren't you going to say something? This is getting kind of awkward, don't you think?

DAWN: You want awkward, I'll give you awkward!

DAWN grabs a pillow and smothers DON's face with it. He begins to struggle – muffled screams.

DON: Are you crazy? Here, you're going to need these tonight.

DON surrenders the pill bottle. DAWN throws them out the door.

Now, why would you do that? We're both going to regret that when you fail to sleep tonight.

DAWN continues to smother DON.

I don't know what the big deal is. I like our life together. I like the monotony. I like the familiarity. I like *Law and Order*. I like you. I like that you're getting older. I like the lines on your face. I like your belly. I like your pink pyjamas. And I like sleeping on Monday nights.

DAWN: And you *love* Veronica next door.

DON: Haven't we already covered this? Let's try not to repeat ourselves.

DAWN finally removes the pillow from DON's face but hits him with it.

DAWN: You are so stupid.

DON: Speak rationally for one second, please.

DAWN: Speak rationally for one second, please.

DON: Sometimes you're such a spoiled brat.

DAWN: Sometimes you're such a spoiled brat.

DON: I'm a stupid idiot.

DAWN: You got that right. As if I was going to fall for that. What am I? Eight years old?

DON: No, you're a beautiful, funny, intelligent, slightly obnoxious 36-year-old, now shut up and let's go to sleep.

DAWN: Now, how hard was that?

DON: Pretty hard, actually.

DAWN: Like hard-hard?

DON: Rock hard.

DAWN: Oh, Don.

They start to kiss and get entangled.

DON: Maybe next Monday I could play your part.

DAWN: Let's not get ahead of ourselves.

DON reaches over and turns out the light.

End of Play.

On the Money
by Debbie Patterson

JILL and DARLENE are having cocktails and catching up.

JILL: Her signature is on our money.

DARLENE: What?

JILL: Her goddamn signature is on our money. She's the deputy fucking Governor of the Bank of fucking Canada. She signs our money.

DARLENE: Carolyn Wilkinson?

JILL: Can you believe it?

DARLENE: Are you sure it's the same Carolyn Wilkinson?

JILL: Oh ho, yes. She hasn't aged a day.

DARLENE: I hate her.

JILL: Do you remember what an idiot she was?

DARLENE: I remember how cute and blond and skinny she was.

JILL: Do you remember that day in sociology class? We were learning about life expectancy and she put up her hand and she actually asked, "So if I live beyond my life expectancy, does that mean I'll live for ever and ever and ever?"

DARLENE: Oh my god, I'd forgotten that. Yeah, she's an idiot.

JILL: And then she got a ninety-seven as a final mark.

DARLENE: Shut up. How did she manage that?

JILL: By asking for extra help from Mr. Ellis.

She mimes a hand job.

DARLENE: Seriously?

JILL: No, of course not. She might get her hands dirty. She'd always play dumb and all the boys fell for it. The men too. Helpless and stupid all through high school and now she's the goddamn Deputy Governor of the Bank of Canada. I could puke.

DARLENE: I bet she's totally unhappy.

JILL: She hasn't had kids. Obviously.

DARLENE: Probably anorexic.

JILL: I have a BA in poli-sci with a minor in economics and an MBA. My marks were in the top 5% of my graduating class. I was the youngest person ever to pass the Foreign Service exam. And where am I? In a fucking cubicle making collections calls for Revenue Canada. I used to have a corner office, I was a team leader for over ten years. But with all the cuts from the Harper government and four mat-leaves I've been pushed down and down and down.

DARLENE: Where's your union?

JILL: The union can protect my salary, but not my position. If I opt for a better position I have to take the salary that goes with it, which is less than what I'm making now. If I just take whatever shit they throw my way, I get to keep my salary. I can retire in five years, I can't afford a salary cut now. I swear to god, collections is the lowest of the low.

DARLENE: Do you have to break people's knees?

JILL: No, only their spirits.

DARLENE: Oh, Jill.

JILL: I'm not even invested in it and it's destroying me. I don't give a shit if people file their taxes. Well okay, actually I do, because I think the tax system – for the most part – is pretty fair. And we're all in this together, a just society provides support to its weakest members and all that shit. But these people I call, they haven't filed their taxes and usually it's because they're just disorganized or in crisis or they're just not very smart.

DARLENE: Like Carolyn.

JILL: Oh, I wouldn't say Carolyn isn't smart. She's clearly very smart. Strategic. A strategic flirt. And you should hear the people in the cubicles beside me, they're fucking horrible. They'll cold call someone, call them for the first time and immediately start treating them like they're a criminal: grilling them on why they haven't filed their taxes, "tax evasion is a very serious offence" "your fines are accumulating daily" "what are you trying to hide?" "you expect me to believe that?" "crying won't help you now." I can't stand listening to them. And I hate being in conflict with people all the time. I refuse to assume the worst about everyone I interact with. And I get shit for it from my thirty-three-year-old "boss" who tells me I need to be more aggressive, the cocky little shit. I try to separate it, I try to say I'm not the one in conflict with these people, I'm just making a phone call. But it doesn't work, I still get stressed out.

DARLENE: Have you tried yoga?

JILL: No time. I'm taking Jesse to ringette and Brownies, Reese has Scouts and hockey. Every night of the week it's just go go go: feed them dinner, take them to their things, go home, bath time, homework, bedtime, wash the dishes, make the lunches, walk the dog, go to bed. I'm too old for this. This second family thing seemed like a good idea at the time. Seriously, at one point I had two in university and two in diapers. What was I thinking?

DARLENE: Good thing you're not the Deputy Governor of the Bank of Canada. Who's got the time for that?

JILL: I'd make time.

DARLENE: You're good, Jill. You don't need your name on our money. You're a great mom, you bring a level of class and civility to Revenue Canada. And you're gorgeous.

JILL: You had me until the gorgeous.

DARLENE: Well, you are.

JILL: So are you.

DARLENE: No no, I've got a great personality, and we all know what that means. I'm trying to cultivate the "large and in charge" persona. I've always had the sense of humour for it, but since being on antidepressants and gaining 100 pounds – literally, 100 pounds in one year – I now have the body and, bonus, the lack of filters to really take it on.

JILL: Wait, antidepressants? This is new.

DARLENE: Yeah, I can't remember when the last time was that we saw each other. I think it was before everyone died.

JILL: Who died?

DARLENE: Well, first my mom, which was really hard. And then I think you met Mickey, the little guy I was fostering.

JILL: No, I think he had just gone back up north when I visited you.

DARLENE: Oh yeah, that was really hard, too. I fostered him for six years, I've been doing medical fostering. He was from Pond Inlet and he was palliative, so he needed to be closer to a big hospital. He was pretty high needs: he couldn't get around, he couldn't really talk, I had to tube feed him, he was on oxygen. It was really intense, you know, like around-the-clock care, which honestly, I found really fun. Oh my god, he was so cute! He would laugh at anything. We had these pet rats that he called puppies, "puh peh" and he loved them. But then one day Children's Aid decided he should go back up north to his parents and six days later he was gone. They just took him.

JILL: No way.

DARLENE: He was my first foster kid and I guess I just didn't get how it worked. I didn't know I wasn't supposed to fall in love. *(Beat.)* So, yeah, he went back to live with his parents, and I would call maybe once a month just to see how he was doing. And it was always kind of awkward, like they didn't want to talk to me, maybe they felt like I was judging them or something, I don't know. So I decided I had to back off a bit, I waited two months before calling. And his mom answered and was like "Why are you calling? He died over a month ago." And I was all "Why didn't you call me?" And she says, "We notified everyone who needed to be notified." That was it.

JILL: Children's Aid didn't let you know?

DARLENE: You read the papers. They have a hard enough time protecting the children, they don't have any time for the foster parents.

JILL: So they hang you out to dry.

DARLENE: That's the gig. And while all that was going on my mom was dying, so it was pretty rough. At least I was able to go be with my mom and look after her, without having to look after Mickey too. You know, if I'm looking for the silver lining. The glass is half-full.

JILL: You're like some kind of saint.

DARLENE: I don't think my kids would agree with you. After my mom died I had all this time on my hands, so I asked my boys what they thought of taking on another foster kid. Adam was like "yeah whatever" but Jack said, "Okay, but could we get one that's not so freaky looking this time?"

JILL: Was Mickey freaky looking?

DARLENE: He was freaking cute! The cutest little freaky looking kid you've ever seen! So then Children's Aid called and they said they had a kid that needed medical fostering, he was really in rough shape. And I was like "bring it on," you know, because I'm really good at that. But I didn't know how to ask "Is he freaky looking?" So I'm asking all these questions, you know, medical questions. And she goes like, "He was in a house fire, he lost his hand, he's still recovering from the burns" so I'm thinking, "okay, a little scarring, maybe a bit freaky." Then she tells me before that he had a stroke, and his left side is paralyzed. So then I'm like, "Hmmm, maybe a bit too freaky looking." But she starts describing to me how this half paralyzed kid was stuck in a burning building and I didn't have the heart to say no.

JILL: Oh no.

DARLENE: And the best part was his name was Goo. I was like "um, how do you spell that?" She goes, "G-O-O." Goo.

JILL: Goo.

DARLENE: Goo Poogootook.

JILL: Poogoo – ?

DARLENE: Goo Poogootook.

JILL: Goo Poodoodook?

DARLENE: Poo-goo-took.

JILL: Poo-goo-took.

DARLENE: Goo...

JILL: Goo...

DARLENE: Goo Poogootook.

JILL: Goo Poogootook.

DARLENE: Brilliant.

JILL: And... Freaky looking?

DARLENE: But so cute! Adam got him a little pirate hat, you know with his droopy eye he kind of looked like a pirate. Then Jack got him a little plastic hook from the dollar store for his hand, or where his hand was supposed to be, I guess. Taught him to say "Arrrrrr!"

JILL: So he could talk?

DARLENE: I'm such a loser. I thought he couldn't talk, but then his dad came down to visit him and they were chatting away in Inuktitut. He could totally talk, I just couldn't understand him. I was like, "Oh, what cute little noises he's making." So ignorant.

JILL: So... Did he go back up north?

DARLENE: No. He died.

JILL: Oh. Sorry.

DARLENE: Yeah, I know. He was palliative when I got him. He was with us for less than a year.

JILL: That must've been so hard.

DARLENE: Yeah, it must've been. I just kind of shut down, stopped going out, went on meds, gained 100 pounds and now, I'm feeling better, I'm not depressed, but I don't want to see anybody I used to know. I've gained a hundred freaking pounds.

JILL: That's ridiculous, Darlene.

DARLENE: I know it's ridiculous. I'm ridiculous. I'm a ridiculous fat lady circus freak who likes taking care of super sick freaky-looking little kids. My life is ridiculous. Maybe I should become a hoarder and be done with it. I'm not depressed anymore, I'm not even sad, I just see the judgy looks in people's eyes and I know they're thinking "loser" and I don't want to deal with it.

JILL: So how come you agreed to see me?

DARLENE: You said you were coming to town for the reunion.

JILL: Yeah, I assumed you would be going.

DARLENE: I'd rather poke my eyes out with a fork.

JILL: Okay.

DARLENE: It's going to be horrible.

JILL: It might be great.

DARLENE: Seriously? You want to hear Carolyn "Airhead" Wilkinson singing "Killing Me Softly" off key at the talent night?

JILL:	Then watch her cry her big fake tears when Michael Didsbury throws a bouquet of roses on the stage.
DARLENE:	Don't put yourself through it. There's no need.
JILL:	Aren't you curious?
DARLENE:	No. I know who's going to be there. The arrogant puffed-up jocks who've bullied their way through life and the Carolyn Wilkinsons who've made a career of flirting with powerful men and saying no. No real person, no one with integrity, no one who lives an authentic life shows up at their thirty-year high school reunion. Unless they're a relentless optimist who always looks for the best in everyone around them.
JILL:	Well then I'll find that person.
DARLENE:	Dummy, you are that person.
JILL:	Busted. You're right. I suck.
DARLENE:	We suck. We both suck equally hard. We don't need those assholes rubbing our noses in how bad we suck.
JILL:	You don't suck, you're a saint. You pour all this love into children that nobody else gives a shit about.
DARLENE:	And you bring humanity to Revenue Canada, which is some kind of freaking miracle. But we have never been the girls that all the guys want to sleep with.
JILL:	No.
DARLENE:	And we never will be.
JILL:	That ship has sailed.
DARLENE:	We never even set foot on the pier.

JILL: And that's what it takes to be the goddamn Deputy Governor of the Bank of Canada.

DARLENE: It sure looks like it.

JILL: Yup.

DARLENE: Yup.

Pause.

Strumming my pain with his fingers...

TOGETHER: ...*singing my life with his words, killing me softly with his song, killing me softly, with his song...*

They continue to sing as lights fade.

End of Play.

The Intersection
by Ellen Peterson

A MAN and a WOMAN, both around forty, give walking tours of a Winnipeg neighbourhood, indicating the major landmarks as they go. There are traffic sounds that diminish as the piece progresses.

MAN: In university I lived in one of those party houses. This is it here: it looks nicer now. It smelled like Sal's all the time, inside and out, from the Sal's across the back lane. I always said, "Oh, but I never eat there," but I ate there all the time, breakfast mostly. It's where I used to meet my dealer, for god's sakes. It was practically his office. Eat breakfast, read the paper, wait for the hangover to pass, get some hash, start all over again. It's so funny now, 'cause your to-do list changes a lot over the years. Even now I smell a nip I get a contact high.

WOMAN: This is a very historical neighbourhood for me, so we might as well start here. Well…right over there, there was a pretty good bar. We went there a lot. All my so-called friends from university: where are they now? I went out with the bartender for a while. Okay, I wanted to. Sometimes it seems like every guy I went out with lived around here. Sometimes it seems like I went out with a lot of guys. What's a lot? I blame the climate. Most of those guys, they were just sort of illogical extensions of kitchen parties and there is absolutely nothing colder than the front seat of a Plymouth Duster in Winnipeg in January. I always heard about people who would get drunk and then not remember anything. No such luck.

MAN: Some of that time I guess I don't remember so well. My buddy Chris used to call himself Mr. Gilbey when he drank. It was supposed to be like a Jekyll and Hyde thing. Gin made him evil. One time we wrestled people to the ground as they came in and forced them to wear orange nail polish. That stuff you remember. And some of these guys I went to university with were geniuses. Real geniuses, in orange nail polish. And nice girls, some of them, and you'd think, "Why are we all behaving like such idiots?" Once in a while I bump into somebody from then and it's like talking to a ghost. Or they're real and I'm the ghost.

WOMAN: Just at the corner here, upstairs, was the first and last restaurant I ever worked at. After that it was a futon store. Or hydroponics? And now it's a law office. My first day I served mouldy bread to a minor local celebrity. God, people take their food so personally! People used to say, I'm not sure if it's still true, that Winnipeg had more restaurants per capita than any other city in North America. You couldn't believe how often people would say that. If you said, "What's the name of that restaurant we went to that time" or "they opened up a futon store where that restaurant used to be" or "god I hate working in this fucking restaurant" somebody would say, "Did you know that Winnipeg has more restaurants per capita…" But if eighty percent of them are crap, why brag about it?

The Intersection by Ellen Peterson

And this is the house where I lost my virginity. I don't go out of my way to come by here. He had a fireplace in his apartment, what was I supposed to do?

MAN: Chris lived in that grey house across the street for a while. It was such a dump. That was the place with the closet door that wouldn't open and depending on his degree of inebriation he would either try to pick the lock or just get shit scared and crash at my place. I don't think there was anything in the closet but it was weird. Weird place for a nice boy from River Heights to end up.

We had this friend Geoff. Everybody was either called Dave or Geoff. Or maybe Mike. Brian. Anyway. Geoff lived in this great house he inherited from his grandmother. This was after university. We played a lot of pool there, watched a lot of movies. Geoff was the first person I knew who had a Betamax. Then Geoff met this girl who hated everybody he knew. That happens a lot. She moved in and redecorated everything, including the inside of his head. We never got invited anymore. That's when I knew I was a grown-up.

WOMAN: Okay. Well. Some bad stuff happened here. This is where I got my heart broken. It was my fault. I was stupid. I don't like talking about it even now. He lived in this crummy building for a while, everybody did. So every time I drive down this street for the rest of my life, that's what I get to think about. And it's not like you can avoid it, it's a major artery.

You know, that's why people leave town. It's not the climate, or the opportunities, unless you're talking about the opportunity not to have to keep running into parts of your life you'd rather forget. Every time I come around a corner, there I am again, way younger, doing something stupid.

Not every time, but enough. Of course it wasn't all bad. Of course not. But this isn't really a young person's kind of town and so to be young here automatically makes you an outsider. You can't win.

MAN: Now on the corner over there is one of those buildings everybody lived in, like a beehive. Either you lived there or you used to or you knew somebody who did and if somebody said, "I live at the corner of such-and-such" everybody'd go "hey that guy that owns the Laundromat where I go used to be married to a woman with a glass eye that lives on the main floor, do you know her?" And they'd be like "yeah, my sister's boyfriend was in a band with her" or something. But years later, years later, after Chris had lived in Vancouver for a while he came back here and we went to a party in this building and that's where he met the woman who got him started on crack and it was all downhill from there. Nothing like watching a prairie boy go downhill. Underground before you know it.

WOMAN: The first time I ever tried to get high was with this friend of mine on the steps of the Ledge. What did they used to call that, Purple City? You were supposed to smoke up, I don't know, hold your breath and look at the skyline upside down and it would turn purple. I never saw it. That friend, she was one of those girls with a cool name that you just knew wasn't on her birth certificate. She doesn't live in Winnipeg anymore, surprise. I moved to Toronto once for about ten minutes but I came back because, well, either you belong somewhere or you don't.

MAN: All that time I was working nights at a Safeway, shipping and receiving. I had this girlfriend and after we broke up I was thinking of leaving town. I couldn't figure out where I'd go. And one night at the end of my shift I go out and the car's dead. I bought that Duster off Geoff just after he met Poison Girl.

WOMAN: After the security guards told us to get off the steps we walked across the bridge and sat around by that fountain that isn't there anymore.

MAN: This should be a winter story with the dead car and everything, but it's not. It was so late there's no buses. But it was nice out, you know? Nice summer night. I decided to walk home, which was far, 'cause I was staying with my brother on MacMillan.

WOMAN: It was so quiet and soft the way the air is in summer. Nobody was around and we sat with our feet in the fountain and smoked cigarettes and talked until we were all out. Then we just sat there.

MAN: And it was quiet, all the houses with everybody sleeping. I'm waiting on the corner by Papa George's there. I hear a couple of girls laughing across the street and a car goes by. I started having déjà vu and I thought: I've been here for a thousand years.

WOMAN: Everything just seemed to be waiting, I don't know what for. When the sun was coming up I walked home over the river, past the Golden Boy and the people sleeping under the trees there. It felt like a different city, only this one was mine.

MAN: I didn't leave. I met another girl and we live in Charleswood. Chris is long gone. Geoff, who knows. Sometimes I think Winnipeg is everybody I miss.

End of Play.

Agony & Ecstasy
by Alix Sobler

Part I

MAGGIE and NICK are cleaning the apartment.

MAGGIE: I can't believe we've been married five years.

NICK: I know.

MAGGIE: It's so nice, because I used to worry a lot about choking to death when I was eating alone.

NICK looks up from what he is doing.

NICK: That *is* nice.

MAGGIE: Yeah, and also that I would go weeks like that, and no one would find me until after the cats had already eaten my face off. I hardly ever have to worry about that anymore.

NICK: Well, it's great to be able to check something off the list.

MAGGIE: Yeah! Although, I guess you do occasionally go away for business.

NICK: That's true.

MAGGIE: But you usually call every night.

NICK: Yeah. Unless I'm out of the country. Then it could be a few days.

MAGGIE: Maybe a week.

NICK: Maybe a week.

MAGGIE: Hm.

They go back to cleaning.

MAGGIE: I guess the important thing is that the cats don't die even though I am not here to feed them.

NICK: Yeah, I would agree that that's the important thing.

MAGGIE: And that they wouldn't eat each other.

NICK: Right.

MAGGIE: And you'd come home eventually. And then just make sure you take them to the vet to make sure there is no damage or vitamin deficiency from eating human flesh.

NICK: Maggie!

MAGGIE: What?

NICK: Are you nuts?

MAGGIE: Why?

NICK: I'm not keeping the cats after they eat your face.

MAGGIE: Why not? It's not their fault I wasn't alive to feed them. They had to eat something!

NICK: Nevertheless.

MAGGIE: So what are you going to do? You're going to give them away?

NICK: No!

MAGGIE: Well, what? *(He looks at her.)* Euthanize them?!

NICK: Well...

MAGGIE: For eating me, when you *know* that's what I would have wanted?

NICK: OK, fine, I won't euthanize them. But I am not keeping them.

MAGGIE: Why not? Then a part of me would always be with you.

NICK: Not only is that really gross, but I think it would be quite upsetting to think about them dining on your dead body every time I look at them. No, I couldn't handle that.

MAGGIE: So you'd be really upset.

NICK: If I came home and found you dead, your face eaten by the cats? Yeah. I think it's safe to say I'd be bummed.

MAGGIE: Honey, that's so sweet.

They go back to cleaning.

Part II

NICK and MAGGIE walk hand in hand in the park.

MAGGIE: Look at that couple.

NICK: Which?

MAGGIE: Those two. The old ones.

NICK: Yeah?

MAGGIE: They're so cute. They're in their 80s and still holding hands.

NICK: So? They'll probably fall down without someone to lean on.

She slaps him playfully and he laughs.

Why do you always call old people cute and feel the need to point them out? They're not Labradors.

MAGGIE: I appreciate them.

NICK: For what? For living a long time?

MAGGIE: I guess.

NICK: OK, but that doesn't really make them cute. When you say that, it's a little…

MAGGIE: What?

NICK: Well, it's a little…condescending.

MAGGIE: No, it's not!

NICK: Yeah, it is.

MAGGIE: Well, it's not meant to be.

NICK: And yet.

MAGGIE: So me expressing my appreciation of them is condescending, but you ignoring them completely is OK?

NICK: Funny how that works.

Pause.

MAGGIE: I hope we're still holding hands when we are that age.

NICK: I probably won't live that long.

MAGGIE: No, probably not. But if you do. *(Pause, snuggling in a bit.)* Aren't you excited to grow old together?

NICK:	Not really.
MAGGIE:	You're not?
NICK:	Excited to grow old?
MAGGIE:	TOGETHER.
NICK:	I mean, I don't really look forward to getting older.
MAGGIE:	But that's not what I'm asking.
NICK:	Isn't it?
MAGGIE:	No.
NICK:	What then?
MAGGIE:	Getting old, together. Isn't that like, the thing? When people get married, commit to each other. Isn't that the trope? "Someone to grow old with."
NICK:	I don't know. Not the biggest part for me.
MAGGIE:	Really?
NICK:	No. *(She looks at him.)* It's just hard for me to get excited about getting old.
MAGGIE:	Huh.

Pause. They both look off in the distance.

NICK:	Look, I guess, I don't want to die, you know, and like, I want to be with you, so I mean. Yeah. Yeah, I guess if I am going to live, and get old, I want us to…you know, not be apart. So in that way, if you look at it, then I guess, yeah, OK. I guess I could sort of look forward to growing old together.

Pause. MAGGIE slowly smiles to herself.

Part III

> *MAGGIE and NICK are hanging out. NICK's phone rings. MAGGIE reacts throughout this phone call.*

NICK: Hello? Oh hi, Mom.

> *MAGGIE rolls her eyes, goes back to thumbing through a magazine or whatever.*

No, nothing new, just hanging around. Mm-hm. No, I didn't see that. In the paper? No, I don't really read the paper. Just online. She won an award? Wow. That's impressive. No, not anymore. Well, not really since prom. Well, that's great, Mom, she always was a smart girl. No. They don't really give out awards for – Uh-huh. No, I know you're not.

> *MAGGIE looks up in disbelief.*

Yes, we've talked about it. We agreed we're not really ready yet. You know how long. Five years. Well, you can't really put a time requirement on these things, Mom, you're either ready or you're not. No. We're not. It's not just Maggie, although, let's be honest, it's a great commitment for her.

> *MAGGIE makes a hanging-herself gesture.*

Yeah, I think she knows that. No, I am not going to tell her that. Because she knows. She *knows* how old she is, Mom. I don't think she needs me to remind her. No, I know you're not.

> *MAGGIE throws down her magazine angrily.*

Next week? Not a whole lot, why? A visit?

> *MAGGIE looks at him with panic.*

I guess, what would you do, book a room at the – Stay with us?

> *MAGGIE approaches him, shaking her head no.*

NICK: We don't have a ton of room. Yes, we still have the pullout in the den.

> *MAGGIE gestures wildly to say "no."*

I suppose...maybe.

> *MAGGIE throws up her arm in frustration.*

For how long, a couple of days? Oh, ten.

> *MAGGIE gets down on her hands and knees begging.*

I mean, um...I can't...I can't think of a reason why not. I really can't.

> *MAGGIE splays out on the floor, utterly defeated.*

Ok, Mom, great. Looking forward to it too. OK, talk to you later, bye.

> *NICK hangs up the phone.*

My mother says hi.

> *NICK exits. Maggie stays on the floor.*

Part IV

> *NICK approaches a very full recycling bin and considers the pop can in his hand. He balances the can at the top of the overflowing pile, house-of-cards style. Satisfied, he sits down again. MAGGIE enters and sees the recycling bin.*

MAGGIE: What is this?

NICK: What?

MAGGIE: This. *(Indicates the bin.)*

NICK: I don't understand your question.

MAGGIE: You don't understand – what's that supposed to mean?

NICK: It means you know very well what that is.

MAGGIE: Do I?

NICK: Yeah, you do. So why are you asking?

MAGGIE: I am asking because it is starting to resemble a conceptual art piece.

NICK: Well, any resemblance to a creative work is strictly coincidental.

MAGGIE: You know, ever since you quit smoking this recycling bin hardly gets emptied.

NICK: That's not true.

MAGGIE: It is true.

NICK: I'll get to it.

MAGGIE: It was almost annoying. No sooner did I drop a scrap of paper in there than you were whisking it away to empty it.

NICK: Oh, please.

MAGGIE: You used to sit and watch me eat yogurt, just waiting for the container.

NICK: I'll get to it.

MAGGIE: Now a mouldy milk carton can sit here for days, you don't even bat an eye.

NICK: You're exaggerating.

MAGGIE: *(Checking out a box in the bin.)* Look at this! I don't even think they make this cereal anymore.

NICK: You know you have two legs that work.

MAGGIE: Excuse me?

NICK: You can take out the recycling, too.

MAGGIE: It's *your* thing.

NICK: Since when?

MAGGIE: Since ALWAYS, Nick.

NICK: Why are you so afraid of change?

MAGGIE: What are you even talking about?

NICK: It was my thing because I used to smoke. But I am not smoking anymore. Did it ever occur to you that every time I have to take the recycling out it's an exercise in temptation?

MAGGIE: No. No, that did not occur to me.

NICK: Well, there you go.

MAGGIE: I have the feeling it's just occurring to you.

NICK: I'm doing really well.

MAGGIE: I'm so happy for you!

NICK: I don't want to jeopardize a relapse.

MAGGIE: For goodness sake.

NICK: I'm just saying.

MAGGIE: What? That it's too much of an emotional struggle to go to the dumpster?

NICK: That you could do it, too.

MAGGIE: Yeah, I could, but I am not going to.

NICK: Why not?

MAGGIE: Because! Because it's your thing!!

NICK: What do you want? You want me to start smoking again?

MAGGIE: No! I want you to take out the recycling!

NICK: I'll get to it!

MAGGIE: Please!

MAGGIE storms out. NICK contemplates the recycling bin for a moment. In a huff he picks it up and exits with it.

Part V

> *MAGGIE and NICK are watching a movie. MAGGIE's phone rings.*

MAGGIE: Hello?

> *NICK picks up the remote and pauses the movie.*

Hi, Cheryl! No, I haven't forgotten, just haven't had a chance. Yeah, let me do that and call you back.

> *She hangs up the phone. NICK picks up the remote and un-pauses the movie.*

Oh, I forgot to tell you –

> *NICK picks up the remote and pauses the movie.*

I told Cheryl and Dave that we would have dinner before the play next week.

NICK: Oh. Sure, great.

> *He un-pauses the movie. After a moment:*

MAGGIE: I do not want to go to that restaurant we went to last time.

> *NICK picks up the remote and pauses the movie.*

NICK: Which time?

MAGGIE: Before the Jets game when that crazy couple was having a fight really loudly?

NICK: It wasn't the restaurant's fault?

MAGGIE: Well, that waitress was a lot more polite than I would have been.

NICK: Well, fine, pick a new place.

MAGGIE: Yeah.

> *Pause. He looks at her. She is deep in thought. He un-pauses the movie.*

It's just hard because Cheryl is vegan now.

NICK pauses the movie.

So where can we go? There's that place on Main… or sushi. But will you be able to eat anything if we go for sushi?

NICK: Yes. I can eat anything anywhere.

MAGGIE: Are you sure? Because it's like a very limiting thing to be vegan.

NICK: No, I understand what it means to be vegan.

MAGGIE: OK, good, I will make a reservation.

NICK un-pauses the movie.

I mean I get the vegan thing. It's the raw food vegans I really don't understand.

NICK attempts to ignore her and keep the movie on. She doesn't notice because she's thinking.

And the whole paleo-diet thing.

NICK sighs and pauses the movie, knowing he's in for it.

I mean, what is that about? Why, why, why would you want to eat like a caveman? Didn't cavemen only live until 30? Didn't they spend literally all their time hunting and gathering? Aren't we supposed to be excited to be able to commit mental energy to other things at this point? I had to make cookies for this raw food guy's birthday at work, and it was the strangest thing. It was just a list of ingredients. It was like, here's a bunch of stuff, now mush it all together. That was it. Those were the cookies. I mean jeez. I am all for being healthy, but there's a limit, you know?

NICK: Yeah. I hear you.

MAGGIE: I mean what would I do if you suddenly wanted to live on a paleo-diet? That would suck. I would be screwed.

NICK: I would never do that to you.

MAGGIE: But someday…

NICK: Never.

MAGGIE: How do you know?

NICK: Some things you just know.

MAGGIE: Yeah, but you can't say never.

NICK: Sure you can. You just do.

MAGGIE: What if you're wrong? What if you feel one way for years and years, practically your whole life, and then you just wake up and you feel differently the next day? Something that you never found bothersome before suddenly bothers the hell out of you.

NICK: Like cooked food?

MAGGIE: For example.

NICK: I can tell you right now, I will want cooked food for the rest of my life. I will never want anything but a steady diet of food that has been passed over a flame. And if I ever find myself eyeballing a chia seed, hemp-heart salad in a way that makes me uncomfortable…I will close my eyes and count to ten. And order a steak.

> *MAGGIE smiles and kisses him on the cheek. They look at each other and she kisses him on the lips. She stands up and takes his hand because they are going to go…you know.*

MAGGIE: Oh sorry, hon, did you want to watch the movie?

NICK: What movie?

> *End of Play.*

Biographies

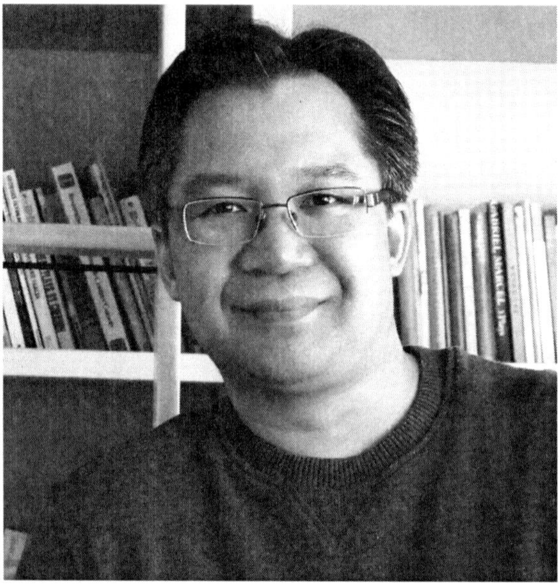

Joseph Aragon (*The Chosen One*)

Joseph Aragon is a Winnipeg playwright and composer. A veteran of the Winnipeg Fringe Theatre Festival, Joseph is a two-time winner of the Harry Rintoul Memorial Award for Best New Manitoban Play. His works include the plays *The Unlikely Sainthood of Madeline McKay* and *How the Heavens Go*, and the hit Fringe musicals *Bloodsuckers!*, *Illuminati*, and *Lucrezia Borgia*. His musical *Bloodless: The Trial of Burke and Hare* received a Dora Mavor Moore Award nomination for Outstanding New Musical. As a composer, arranger, and sound designer, he has worked on several Winnipeg productions, including *Jabber and Danny, King of the Basement* for Manitoba Theatre for Young People, and *Ordinary Days* for Winnipeg Studio Theatre. He is a Playwriting graduate of the National Theatre School of Canada and a member of the PTE Playwrights Unit.

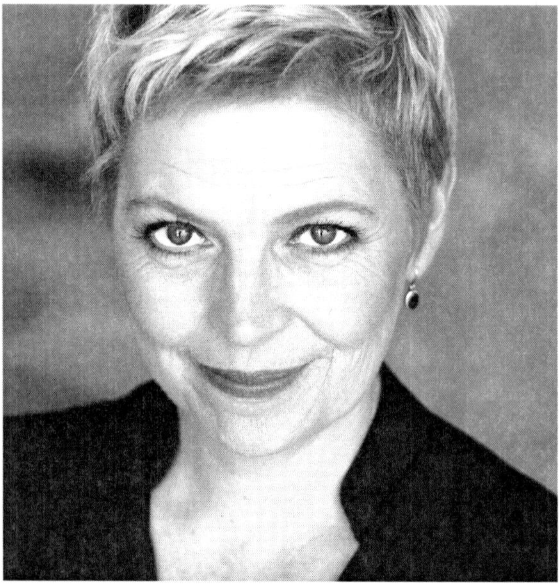

Sharon Bajer (*Chess*)

An actress, playwright and director, Sharon Bajer has been a member of the PTE Playwrights Unit for 10 years where her full-length plays *Molly's Veil* and *Burnin' Love* had their premieres. *Molly's Veil* has had subsequent productions at Western Canada Theatre, The Ottawa Little Theatre, Festival Antigonish and The Curtain Club Theatre. It is published by Scirocco Drama and was nominated for the Eileen McTavish Sykes Award for Best New Book. She has also written *Let Them Howl* for The Nellie McClung Foundation, *Scrabble From the Apple* for Winnipeg Jewish Theatre, and *Hersteria* for Winnipeg Studio Theatre. Sharon has been a regular contributor to the CSF Short Shots, having penned 10 of them and directed many more! sharonbajer.com

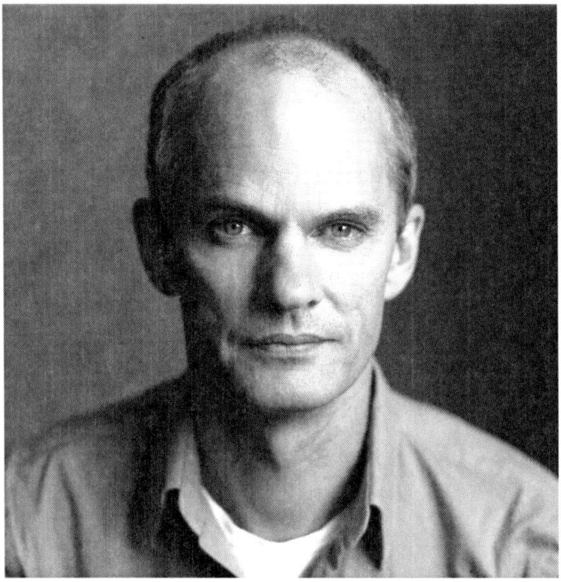

Rick Chafe (*Rage: A Love Story*)

Rick Chafe is a member of the Playwrights Unit at PTE where his two most recent plays were commissioned and produced – *Marriage: A Demolition in Two Acts* and *The Secret Mask* – as well as five short shots and his first professionally produced play, *Talk to Me, Talk to Me*, co-written with Bruce McManus and Norm Dugas about, oh, say thirty years ago. Other plays include *Shakespeare's Dog* (Royal Manitoba Theatre Centre, National Arts Centre, Alberta Theatre Projects), *The Odyssey* (Shakespeare in the Ruins, Two Planks and a Passion, Driftwood), and *Beowulf* (Two Planks and a Passion). Rick is currently working on new commissions for PTE, Theatre Projects Manitoba, and One Trunk Collective. Rick has written and produced for television, documentary, educational TV, radio, and film. The movie musical *Strike!*, co-written with Danny Schur, is shooting this summer for release in 2019. Rick has been nominated for the Siminovitch Prize and The Governor General's Literary Award for Drama for *The Secret Mask*. He lives in Winnipeg with his wife, Martine, their daughter, Charlotte, and two cats.

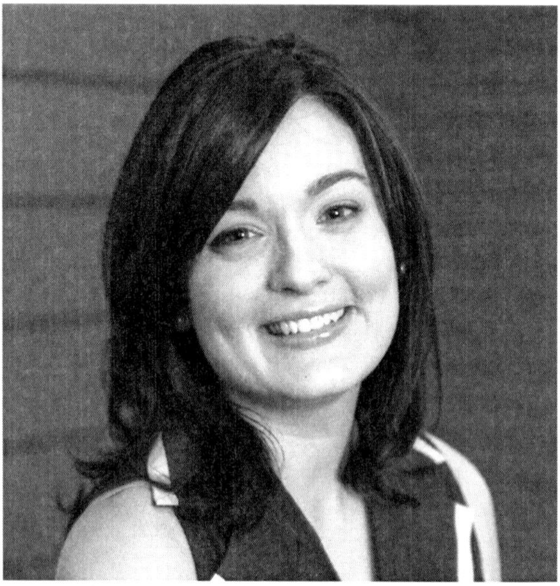

Ginny Collins (*The Propeller Moment*)

Ginny Collins is a Winnipeg-based playwright who has worked with both English and French theatres. Most recently, Ginny's play *The Flats* was produced by Prairie Theatre Exchange as part of their 2016/2017 season. The play was then translated into French (*Les Flats*) and produced at Théâtre Cercle Molière during the same season. In 2014, her play *Good Intentions* was produced at the Winnipeg Jewish Theatre. Ginny's one-act play *The Good Daughter* was published in the *Breakout* anthology of Manitoba playwrights and enjoyed a sold-out run at the Winnipeg Fringe Festival where it was awarded Best of the Fest. Ginny's short play *Terroristas* was also published by Scirocco Drama in a collection of plays for female actors called *Generation NeXXt*. Ginny's other plays include *Prairie Spirits* (2009 Winnipeg Fringe Festival) and *MBTV: Histoire en Direct* – a bilingual play for young audiences. She is a member of the Playwrights Unit at Prairie Theatre Exchange where she is currently under commission for a play called *Revenge and Co.*

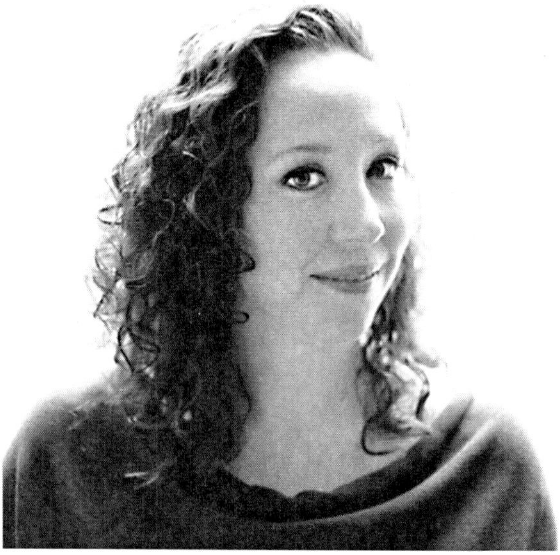

Trish Cooper (*Life of Pie*)

A Theatre graduate from the University of Winnipeg, Trish Cooper has worked as an actor and a writer in Winnipeg and Toronto. She began writing sketch comedy with the Royal Liechtenstein Theatre Company and wrote plays for Fringe festivals across Canada, including *The Comment Card* and *Homely Woman #2*. Trish was a writer/performer for Theatre Projects Manitoba's inaugural In the Chamber series and was a regular contributor for CBC's *Definitely Not the Opera*. *Social Studies*, which Trish developed during her time in the Prairie Theatre Exchange (PTE) Playwrights Unit, is her first full-length play. It was originally produced at PTE in Winnipeg and then received productions at the Centaur Theatre in Montreal and the Firehall Arts Centre in Vancouver. *Social Studies* was published by Scirocco Drama in 2017 and won the Best Manitoba Play at the Manitoba Book Awards. She created a hospital drama for television that is being developed by Farpoint Films. She is now working on her second play commissioned by PTE called *Children's Special Services*.

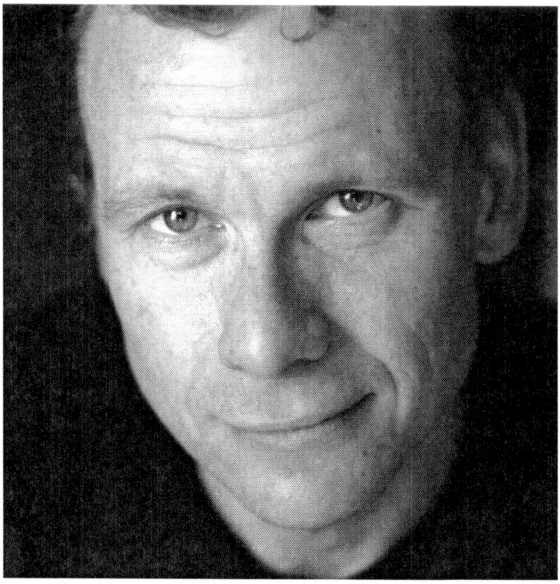

James Durham (*Preparing for Field Day*)

James Durham's plays include *Franklin*, *My Old Man*, and *Cruel and Unusual Punishment*, and *Seeing Red*, *The Big League*. James is currently working on a commission for Prairie Theatre Exchange, entitled *Nothing Like Love*.

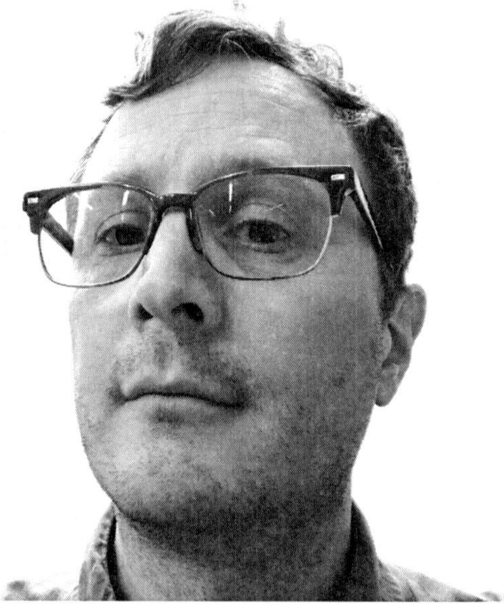

Jason Neufeld (*The Routine*)

Jason Neufeld has worn many theatrical hats throughout his adolescent and adult life. He started out as an actor in high school and university productions which climaxed with numerous (but not too numerous) professional appearances on Winnipeg stages. His love of the stage led to writing and producing his own plays for Fringe festivals, which he toured all across Canada. The success of these shows culminated in being invited to join Prairie Theatre Exchange's Playwrights Unit. After a short stint helping manage the Winnipeg Fringe Theatre Festival, he moved to New York City with his wife and two cats where he managed Young Jean Lee's Theatre Company before finally landing on Broadway, where he currently works in the finance department of a leading Broadway management office.

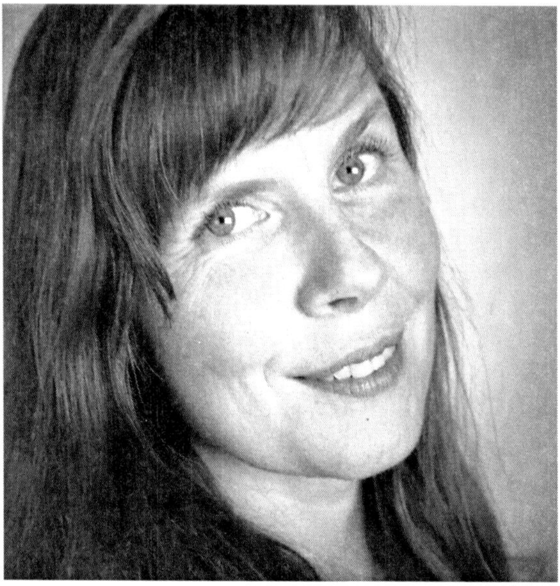

Debbie Patterson (*On the Money*)

Debbie Patterson is a Winnipeg playwright, director and actor. Trained at the National Theatre School of Canada, she is a founding member of Shakespeare in the Ruins (SIR), served as Theatre Ambassador for Winnipeg's Cultural Capital year, was the Carol Shields Writer in Residence 2012 at the University of Winnipeg and Playwright in Residence at Theatre Projects Manitoba in 2013/14. She serves as Artistic Associate at Prairie Theatre Exchange and is currently a member of the PTE Playwrights Unit. Playwriting credits include *Sargent & Victor & Me*, the musical *Head*, and *Molotov Circus*. Directing credits include *Festen* for PTE@PTE, *Midsummer Night's Dream*, *Macbeth* and *Taming of the Shrew* for SIR, *The Crackwalker* for Sweet and Salty Collective and *Saint Joan* for Theatre by the River. As a performer, some of her favourite roles have included Zoya in *Molotov Circus*, the Nurse in *Romeo and Juliet*, Jenny in *Threepenny Opera*, and Jilly in *Sargent & Victor & Me*. In 2016, Debbie became the first physically disabled actor to play Richard III in a professional Canadian production. Debbie is active in the dance community, collaborating on projects with Winnipeg's Contemporary Dancers, Royal Winnipeg Ballet School's Aspirant Program and Young Lungs Dance Exchange. She was honoured with the United Nations Platform for Action Committee's 2014 Activist Award and the Winnipeg Arts Council Making a Mark Award in 2017. She is a proud advocate for disability arts through her work with her company Sick + Twisted Theatre. She lives in Winnipeg with her family: Arne MacPherson, Gislina Patterson and Solmund MacPherson.

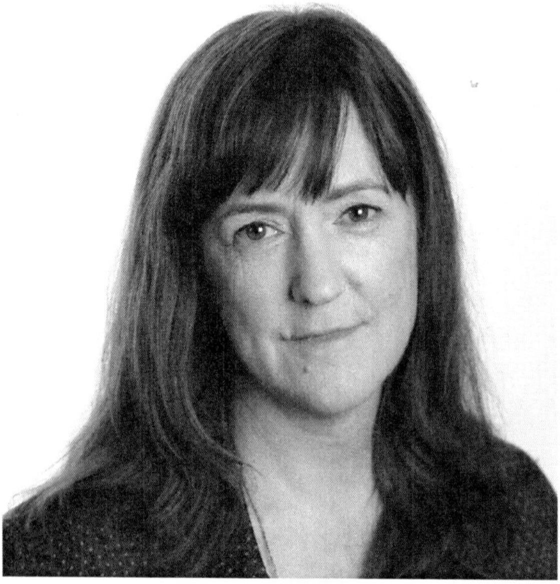

Ellen Peterson (*The Intersection*)

Ellen Peterson is a playwright, dramaturg, actor, and teacher. She is a graduate of the University of Winnipeg (B.A. Theatre '84). Ellen's plays *The Brink* and *The Eight Tiny Reindeer of the Apocalypse* premiered at Prairie Theatre Exchange (2013) and Theatre Projects Manitoba (2012) respectively. Other plays include *Branta Canadensis, Learning to Drive,* and *The Blanket Show,* and *The Goose,* which was read at the 2017 Carol Shields Festival of New Works. As an actor Ellen has appeared on every stage in Winnipeg and in most of the school gyms in Manitoba. Highlights include *Marion Bridge* (PTE), *Over the Tavern* (RMTC), and *Baloney!* (MTYP). Her adaptation of Jane Austen's *Sense and Sensibility* will premiere at the Royal Manitoba Theatre Centre in October 2018. When not writing, Ellen teaches theatre and creative writing. She has served as dramaturg for the Manitoba Association of Playwrights, the Playwrights Atlantic Resource Centre, and the Saskatchewan Playwrights Centre.

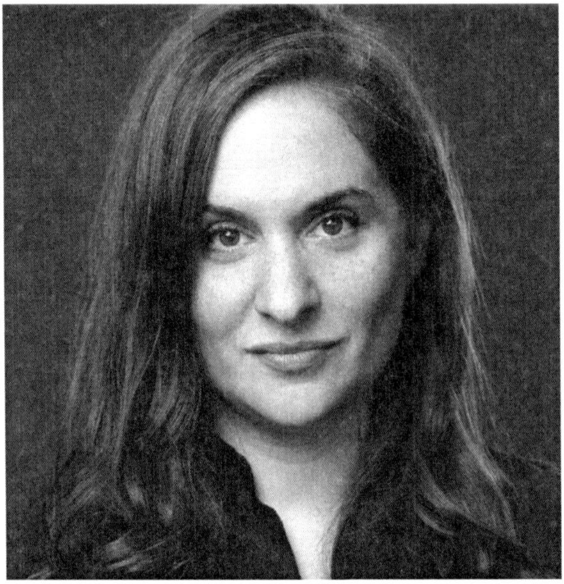

Alix Sobler (*Agony & Ecstasy*)

Playwright and performer Alix Sobler has won the Alliance/Kendeda National Graduate Playwriting Competition and the Canadian Jewish Playwriting Competition, and her plays have been finalists for the O'Neill New Play Conference, the Henley Rose Playwriting Competition and the Jane Chambers Award. She has had work read or produced at the Roundabout Theater Company (New York, NY), South Coast Repertory (Costa Mesa, CA), The Royal Manitoba Theatre Centre (Winnipeg, MB), the Finborough (London, UK), The Segal Centre (Montreal, QC), Brown Trinity Playwrights Rep (Providence, RI), among others. BA: Brown University, MFA: Columbia University. Find more at alixsobler.com.

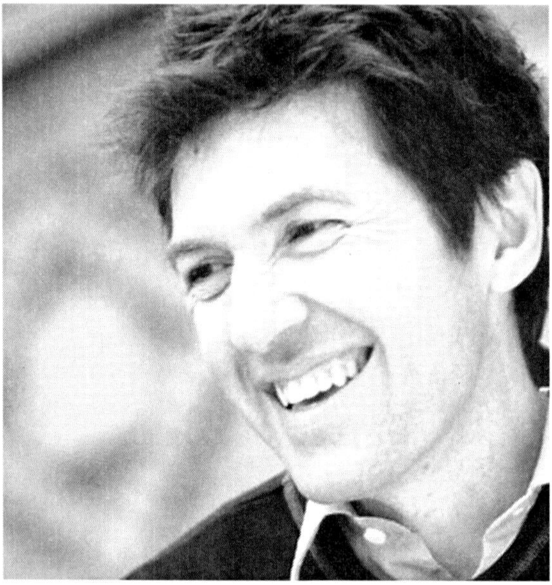

Brian Drader (Editor)

Brian Drader is a writer, dramaturg, actor, and artistic administrator. His plays have been produced in Canada, the United States, and Europe. Awards for his writing include the Herman Voaden National Playwriting Award, the Philadelphia Brick Playhouse New Play Award, and the Lambda Literary Award for Drama (USA), as well as nominations for the Governor General's award and the McNally Robinson Book of the Year. Published work includes *The Norbals, Prok* and *Liar* (Scirocco Drama), and *Curtsy* and *To Be Frank* (Signature Editions). A short film, *Iris And Nathan*, won the National Screen Institute Drama Prize. Commercial engagements include writing the audio components for *Indiana Jones and the Adventure of Archaeology* (with Jodi Essery) and video components for *Star Wars Identities*, both touring museum exhibitions (gsmprjcts/Lucas Films/National Geographic), dramaturg for Cirque du Soleil's *MJ ONE* at the Mandalay Bay in Las Vegas, and dramaturgical support for the 2017 revamp of The Canadian Museum of History in Ottawa. Brian served as the Director of Playwriting at the National Theatre School of Canada in Montreal from 2004 to 2017, and is now the Executive Director of the Manitoba Association of Playwrights.